Service Excellence in Organizations

Service Excellence in Organizations

Eight Key Steps to Follow and Achieve It

Volume I

Fiona Urquhart

BEP BUSINESS EXPERT PRESS

Service Excellence in Organizations: Eight Key Steps to Follow and Achieve It, Volume I

First published in 2019 by
Business Expert Press, LLC
222 East 46th Street, New York, NY 10017
www.businessexpertpress.com

ISBN-13: 978-1-63157-701-7 (paperback)
ISBN-13: 978-1-63157-702-4 (e-book)

Business Expert Press Service Systems and Innovations in Business and Society Collection

Collection ISSN: 2326-2664 (print)
Collection ISSN: 2326-2699 (electronic)

Cover and interior design by Exeter Premedia Services Private Ltd., Chennai, India

First edition: 2019

10 9 8 7 6 5 4 3 2 1

Printed in the United States of America.

Dedication

This book is dedicated to Dr. Don Watts, a beloved friend, an inspirational teacher, and the first person who made me love learning. His field of academic study was a long way from mine, but he captured my imagination and gave me the greatest gift—belief in myself. Sadly, he died a week before I completed the book, but his memory lives in the book and in my heart.

Abstract

This book is structured in two volumes. Volume I deals with the basic tenets of service excellence, while Volume II suggests mechanisms, tools, and techniques to help embed to excellence as the foundation of value that the organization delivers. Both contain practical examples used by some of the companies we know and love; both also contain a self-assessment diagnostic tool that enables organizations to identify where they have built significant strengths in terms of service excellence and where opportunities to enhance their operations exist.

In this first volume, the first chapter introduces the distinction between customer service and service excellence and some of the drivers behind this. The way in which the brand acts to draw the customer into a relationship is covered in the second chapter. The third chapter explores aspects of the customer, their behavior, and experience that any organization needs to understand intimately in order to be able to offer a sensitive and responsive service. A huge element of effective service provision and relationship building is trust, and this is the subject of the fourth chapter. The fifth and the final chapter addresses the quality aspects of service and the way in which some organizations regularly go above and beyond expectations to delight their customer, keep them coming back, and make them rave about the experience they have in their relationships with the organization.

Keywords

customer delight; brand engagement; service drama; servicescape; customer activity cycle; brand authenticity; customer relationship management; loyalty; advocacy; partnering; customer lifetime value; touchpoints; product/service lifecycle; change drivers; innovation; design thinking; service development; service blueprint; service dominant logic

Contents

Chapter 1   Introduction to Service Excellence 1

Chapter 2   Entice 13

Chapter 3   Ensure Quality..49

Chapter 4   Establish Trust 69

Chapter 5   Exceeding Customer Needs and Expectations...............107

About the Author...137

Index 139

CHAPTER 1

Introduction to Service Excellence

We all know what good service is, don't we? We certainly know bad service when we encounter it, which sadly happens all too often. Bad service leaves us feeling disappointed, frustrated, and undervalued. The likelihood that we would seek out that experience again is remote, so we do not return to the company; we feel aggrieved and need to *sound off* about it. Time was, we would have done so to a few friends and family (research says up to 20 people (ACSI survey 1994), and our grievances would have had a very short half-life. Today, we are more inclined to do our complaining online, via Facebook, LinkedIn, Twitter, or a host of other social networking sites, or on a personal blog. The potential for damage is greater than ever; the electronic record, once created, acquires a life of its own and will come up in searches for years to come. The digital world has extended the decay of disgruntled customer stories into eternity.

So much for poor customer service; the new kid on the block is service excellence. What does that mean from a customer perspective? Well, outstanding customer service for sure! But, that is a small part of service excellence. In fact, a better name would be simply excellence. It can apply to organizations, large and small, and in service or in manufacturing sectors; it works across all functions and all levels of personnel. Unlike earlier service and quality initiatives, service excellence blends process and philosophy and imbues companies that espouse it with a charming sprinkling of magic dust that makes them a joy to do business with and creates loyal customers who act as advocates for your organization by telling friends and family how good you are!

When the words service excellence are mentioned, the usual response is "Oh, of course, we have been doing that for years, all of our staff have regular customer service training." People hear the word *service*; they miss the concept of *excellence*. Yet, there is a world of difference! Customer

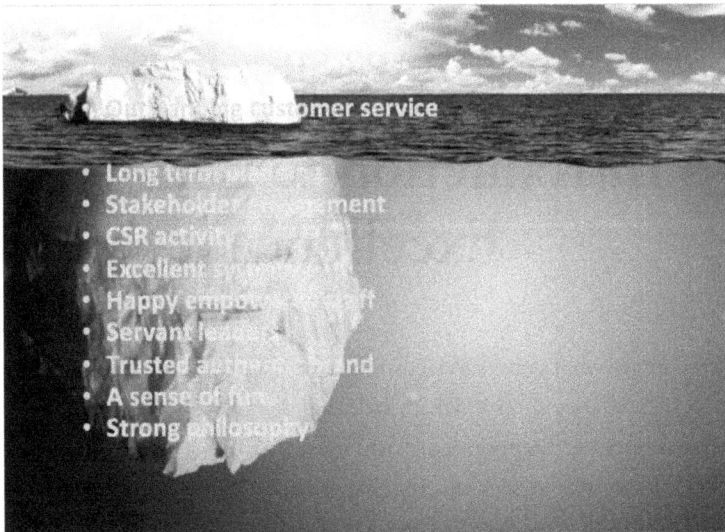

Figure 1.1 The service excellence iceberg

service is, of course, a vital aspect of excellence, but, in exactly the same way as advertising is the tip of the marketing iceberg, customer service is the most visible part of service excellence.

Understanding how to approach service excellence is a bit like knowing how to peel an onion; the answer is *from the outside-in*; conventional business wisdom always starts by looking at internal capabilities—the model taught in business schools worldwide and known as a SWOT analysis is a classic example of this. The S and W are internal strengths and weaknesses, respectively, and only when these have been explored are the external opportunities and threats examined. Businesses must look at themselves from the outside-in, if they are to avoid marketing myopia, and effectively read the emerging themes in their market. A better framework is TOWS, which follows this outside in thinking, taking external factors into account before then matching internal capabilities to opportunities and threats.

Most models for excellence look at the organizational approach and not the customer, and yet, it is the customer who decides which brands to support, and therefore, it is their perspective that should carry weight. The organizational perspective tends to be very much a process designed to assure excellence, and yet, it is quite possible for a very efficient service process to be a lackluster affair, which fails to delight customers.

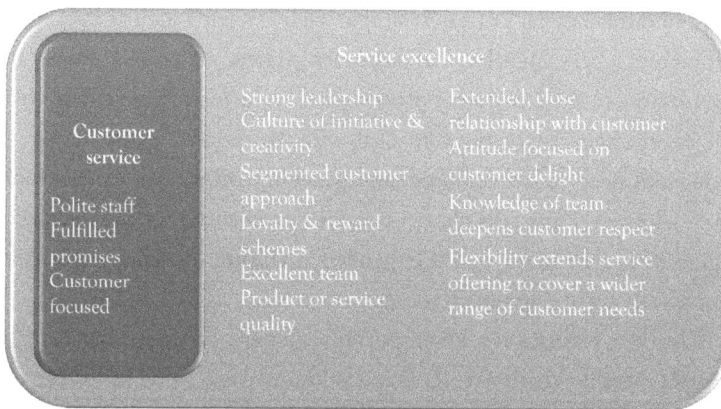

Figure 1.2 Customer service as a subset of service excellence. It is business, but not as we know it

In Aronofsky's haunting 2010 film, Black Swan, the Ballet Director, Thomas Leroy, tells his principal dancer Nina:

"Perfection is not just about control; it is also about letting go."

Despite Nina's painstaking years of training perfecting her technical competences, her performance does not reach her desired level of perfection until she is able to open her heart to feel passion and engage with her audience. Then she shines!

Organizations too can devote years of attention to techniques, which will make them very good performers, but it is not until they are able to engage passionately with their customers through their staff that they earn the accolade of excellence. Organizations known for service excellence are characterized by eight attributes based on the work done by Gareth Morgan and David Mercer in the 1990s. These attributes are:

- Bias for action
- Close to the customer
- Autonomy and entrepreneurship
- Productivity through people
- Value-driven
- Consistency of strategy
- Simple form
- Lean staff
- Simultaneous loose tight properties

Sound managerial processes, supported by systems such as ISO 9000, can deliver a very high level of customer service, which will enable the organization to meet customer expectations in the majority of cases. There will be mechanisms in place to deal with exceptions, where things go wrong and need to be recovered, and generally, things will run as clockwork. However, this falls short of service excellence. Service excellence begins with a mission, which engenders a culture of delighting, rather than merely satisfying the customer.

Clearly, processes are an important element of delivering delight, because meeting customer needs is the foundation stone of excellence. The solid foundation stones provided by efficient processes form a structure on which to create customer delight. Excellence is the pinnacle of a hierarchy, which starts with a solid understanding of the customers the organization serves, enabling an accurate process of segmentation, targeting and positioning to deliver the appropriate quality and type of products and services for the customer segments. Communication with customer segments is initiated by a brand that speaks their language, in a relevant manner. All of these aspects can be achieved through detailed research, sound strategic planning, and good management of creative agencies. And, the mix of these things will deliver a quality of product or service that will effectively meet the needs of the customers and ensure customer satisfaction. This process focus, though, rarely has customers clamoring for more, or raving on a blog about their delight. That must be inspired by the spontaneity of confident, happy people with the right attitude.

Management theory has undergone considerable evolutions over the last 100 years or so, as the following figure shows. It progressed from a production orientation, with management focused on task efficiency and cost reduction, through a focus on human capital, into time and motion studies, development of functional roles, and information systems support. At the same time came a realization that the focus for success should be the customer. Each of these thought evolutions has been jump-started by discontinuous world events—two world wars, the oil crisis, and financial market crashes that forced organizations to think differently about their approach.

Current management thinking is more open and exploratory, allowing the external environment to influence strategy. Understanding customer

	Approach	Central theme	Approximate time period
			1910 · 1920 · 1930 · 1940 · 1950 · 1960 · 1970 · 1980 · 1990 · 2000 · 2010 · 2020
	Scientific management	Quest for best approach to task	
	General administration theorists	Analysis of manager role & good practice	
	Human resources	Understanding employee behaviour seen as key to successful management	
	Quantitative	Improve decision quality by measuring decision variables	
	Process	Creation of functional management roles	
	Systems	Interconnection	
	Contingency	Depends what you want to achieve. Strong leadership	
Holistic approach	Excellence	Customer is the standing point, everyone markets the organisation, Culture of excellence pervades top down	
Business orientation	Partnership orientation	Let's work with our customers to improve what they do/want to do	
	Relationship orientation	Let's understand our customers needs and make what they want	
	Marketing orientation	What kind of widgets might the market need?	
	Sales orientation	How can we sell more widgets?	
	Production orientation	Let's make as many widgets as possible	
Discontinuous world events driving business responses			WW1 WW2 Vietnam Oil shock Bank

Figure 1.3 Evolution of the management theory and business orientation

needs is seen as paramount. So, management focus and business orientation are coalescing in the holistic approach of service excellence. Service excellence has cherry picked the best aspects of each approach to produce a blend of good solid scientific performance measurement with the charm of serendipity and passion humanizing the process. This produces authentic organizations offering a service to customers that is especially relevant, totally superior, and sufficiently unusual that it gets people talking about it and returning for more!

Service Excellence Overview

Excellence works from the outside in—ensuring the customer perspective is at the heart of strategy—the EEEEEEE model. The process begins with branding to *entice* the customer by making a brand promise, *ensuring quality* is the internal meeting of that promise, *exceeding customer needs and wants* helps *establish trust*, and the organization can then *embed* loyalty by *energizing, exciting, and elating*, allowing it to *extend* the offering in new directions, and ensure the customer can responsibly deal with any a residue from product use.

This customer focus and other approaches are outlined using relevant theory and latest academic concepts. It goes on to explain how to embed it into your own organization, using selected models as a framework. Hence, it falls into two areas: observational or case study with lessons learned section at the end of each chapter that feed into the implementation section that offers models, checklists, frameworks for problem identification and successful pragmatic solutions.

Service excellence is a culmination of various initiatives and thinking within business and operational management. However, it is firmly focused on placing the customer perspective at the heart of the business operations and unites production quality, relationships, branding, robust strategies into a winning, sustainable, and future-proofed approach.

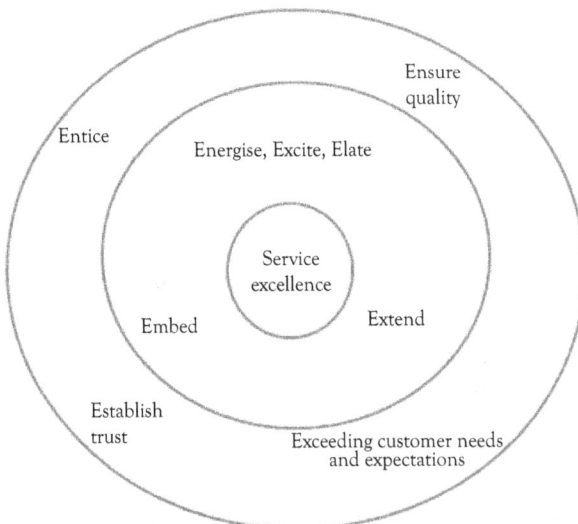

Figure 1.4 7 Es of service excellence

Historically, businesses focused on the organizational perspective then became more customer-focused. As the environment became more competitive, this moved from a sellers' to a buyers' market, and hence from a production to marketing orientation. Service excellence moves things to the next stage, recognizing a number of truisms:

- The easiest part to change of the business system you are in is your own organization and its mindset, so you need to understand the environment and its trajectory first.
- If what you do does not appeal to customers, nothing else matters.
- Good quality service makes happy customers, happy customers make happy staff, happy staff make happy customers.
- Happy customers return, become ambassadors, deliver more profits.
- Loyalty, profitability, caring for all stakeholder groups create a more robust and durable business.

Service excellence is being hailed as a panacea for organizations; yet, there is universal confusion as to what it means, and all models so far take a corporate systems-based perspective, which goes against the grain of excellence. Also, the name service excellence leads to the assumption that it equates with customer service, rather than the holistic, strategic competitive advantage it actually creates. Managers on the ground have the feeling that they are trying to grasp a jelly—it looks good until you start trying to do something with it, then it loses structure, and disintegrates.

This book gives an accessible explanation and an actionable structure. It starts with the dynamic context of the world in which businesses operate, to ensure that the organization understands that it is business trends and customers that shape opportunities, threats, and demands, rather than the business itself. It then focuses on what is important to the customer, and gives organizations a customer tinted lens through which to understand their operations. Against this very external backdrop, it offers a model to embed excellence in the internal daily practices so that organizations can color match between the customers dream and actual reality.

It acknowledges the need for a model that intertwines four strands: process, philosophy, people, and sustainability. No single strand is strong enough as a standalone; it is the fusion of these strands that brings the strength and future success. These seemingly disparate aspects of management combine to produce an organization that is truly excellent from any perspective.

Excellence businesses are open hearted to social causes, encouraging staff to become involved for their own development and well-being, as well as bringing new ideas from other environments, and refreshing creativity in staff members. Open minded, they look to collaborate rather than compete, and overall, they seek win–win opportunities by collaboration with a wide range of stakeholders. Innovation happens naturally, using cross-functional teams to create *hot spots* where experimentation and creativity flourish to keep the organizations and their service offerings fresh and relevant. Service excellence can be seen as a journey or a destination; truly excellent companies are likely to favor the journey concept, as this acknowledges the principle of continual improvement.

Service excellence businesses are profitable—up to 20 percent more so than other businesses; they are also outstanding organizations to work for. Perhaps, that combination is not so surprising. They buck the familiar paradigm of businesses jealously guarding their strategy, conserving their profits, and looking inwardly.

The Benefits of a Service Excellence Approach

Building loyalty makes sense on so many levels and for so many business functions. It can raise income and reduce costs:

- Existing customers are easier to market to because they already know you. You can sell more of the same, or something else—marketing costs fall.
- The repeat sale is easier because most of the groundwork is done, so selling costs fall.
- Selling to existing customers gives staff the opportunity to build relationships, have more fun, less stress, more success, so staff are more inclined to stay with the organization—recruitment and training costs fall.
- You know the customer pays promptly—bad debts fall.
- Once a customer account is set up, it only needs maintenance—administration costs fall.

- Loyal customers become advocates telling friends and associates about you—advertising costs fall.

Excellence isn't about working extra hard to do what you're told. It's about taking the initiative to do work you decide is worth doing.
—Seth Godin: Poke the Box

How This Book Is Designed to Work

The book uses sound academic research and principles to underpin a consideration of an organization in terms of its service delivery. It combines this research together with practical business examples to illustrate the points made. It carries the theory forward into a practical analysis and implementation guide.

End of Chapter Review Questions

Strategic issues	Show as a spectrum					
Sustainable competitive advantage (SCA)	High/Low					
What actions do you take to ensure a sustained competitive advantage?						
Differentiation-based SCA						
How frequently do you introduce new products?						
To what extent do you differentiate products?						
How broad is your product line?						
To what extent do you do market research?						
Low cost-based SCA						
Do you have lower production costs than the rest of your industry?						
Are you using the most up-to date production equipment?						
Are you using the most up-to date production techniques?						
Do you look regularly at improvements to layout?						
Do you look regularly at improvements to capacity utilization?						
Do you undertake raw material analyses?						
Do you look at improving raw material access?						

Strategic issues	Show as a spectrum						
Long-term focus	High/Low						
Do you scan your environment?							
Do you do scenario planning?							
What planning horizons do you have?							
What is the average product lifecycle for your sector?							
Do you use social media to monitor customer reactions?							
Are quarterly profits the primary objective?							
Does the organization require rapid payback?							
Do you use any of the following robust strategies? • Branding • Relationship management • Lobbying • Quality programs							
Profitability							
How does your profitability compare with your industry?							
Is profitability rising?							
Is profitability evenly spread across product or service lines?							
Do you measure profitability market by market?							
Is there an emphasis from top management on market performance?							
Do all products or services have to be profitable?							

How well do you interact with stakeholders?		
Do you do regular stakeholder audits?	Yes	No
Do you have a strategy for managing stakeholders?		
Do you engage with your community?	Yes	No
Do you encourage your people to be involved with other stakeholders?	Yes	No
Are you involved in industry-level bodies?	Yes	No
Are you open to enquiries from students, universities and so on?	Yes	No
Do you track outcomes of impromptu stakeholder encounters?	Yes	No
Is corporate social responsibility important to your organization?	Yes	No
Do you engage with your employees' families?	Yes	No

References

Bhargava, R. 2008. *Personality Not Included.* McGraw Hill.

Godin, S. 2011. *Poke the Box.* Do you Zoom Inc.

Gronroos, C. 2007. *Service Management and Marketing.* Wiley.

Kim, W.C., and R. Mauborgne. 2010. *Blue Ocean Strategy.* Barnes & Noble.

Macgregor, D. 1960. *The Human Side of Enterprise.* New York, NY. McGraw Hill.

Mercer, D. 1988. *Marketing Strategy: The Challenge of the External Environment.* The Open University.

Morgan, G. 1988. *Riding the Cutting Edge of Change.* San Francisco: Jossey Bass.

Ouchi, W.G. 1981. *Theory Z: How American Business can Meet the Japanese Challenge.* Reading, Mass: Addison Wesley.

CHAPTER 2

Entice

Chapter Objectives

- To outline the role branding plays for company, staff, and customer and its link to service excellence
- To offer frameworks for the development of engaging brands
- To suggest ways of using the brand throughout the consumer decision-making process to strengthen the customer relationship
- To understand the role that core values play in brand development
- To offer suggestions for surfacing the core values

Chapter Profile

The brand plays a key role as the starting point for marketing communications that entice customers and reward the brand–customer relationship. Creating a brand that customers will find appealing depends on establishing a meaningful relationship, which needs nurturing and developing over time through meaningful customer dialogue. Branding strategies (brand elements, authenticity, and values) determine what the brand stands for, what it looks like, sounds like, or smells like. Effective branding needs to address the core target audience with messages and hooks that appeal to them in their language. Key questions that need addressing are:

- Who are your customers—your success lies in their hands but how can you know what they want?
- How can you get into customer minds and motivations, and how can you attract them?

- How can the brand help in maintaining a loyal relationship with customers?
- How can the brand support existing customers in becoming brand advocates?
- How can your brand attract and retain the right kind of staff for your brand image?
- What depth and intensity is your relationship?
- How can you future-proof your brand and relationship proposition with customers?
- What do you stand for from an ethical and corporate social responsibility perspective?
- How can segmentation, targeting, and positioning add relevance?
- How can you keep the brand fresh and remain current?

The Role of the Brand

Brands, whether as advertisements, in our shops, our homes, or, sadly, as rubbish in our streets, and worse, in our countryside, are part of our lives, and most of us have a love–hate relationship with them as a consequence.

Branding began as a means for cattle and sheep farmers to identify their animals from those of their near neighbors. The old English word means *burning stick*; as long ago as 2700 BC, a hot metal stick was used to mark livestock to indicate ownership and avoid theft. Product manufacturers emulated this by marking their goods, differentiating their (often commodity) goods in a competitive market place. The formal term, and defined process for, came in 1960, from the American Marketing Association.

> *Brand is a name, term, sign, symbol or design, or a combination of them intended to identify the goods and services of one seller or group of sellers and to differentiate them from those of other sellers.*
> —American Marketing Association

Branding helps organizations create a unique, positive character for the product under consideration in the minds of intended target audience. Effectively done, this requires a strategy that is integral to the organization and encompasses every customer touchpoint that in turn evokes more brand awareness. In effect, far exceeding its initial identification role, the brand supports the potential customer, new customer, loyal customer, and lapsed customers throughout their decision-making process. It also attracts and engages suitable people to work in the organization, known as the employer brand, and evaluated on websites such as LinkedIn. The employer brand is rapidly becoming an important aspect of competitive edge for brand owners.

Attracting a customer in the first instance is a key part of what a brand is designed to do and shares a role with a picture and profile on a dating website. Prospective dates and potential customers need a method of evaluating the available options. In either event, people prefer to form a relationship with a person or brand that has character, appeal, shared values, and standards to their own. A great brand will suggest the things that it stands for. This might include tradition, quality, ethical approach, or a range of other aspects; importantly, these need to be designed to meet the characteristics of the chosen target market or the target market selected according to the nature of the product values.

From the first point of engagement with the brand, there is a role to play in supporting the customer through the decision-making process, as shown in the following figure:

The Loyalty Loop

The linear decision-making process has been accepted as the process customers undergo in making purchases (with a few amendments along the way) for several decades. Now, however, the importance of customer retention to profitability is more widely recognized, and a recent paper by management consultants McKinsey has identified the benefits that derive to consumers too.

Actually, the decision-making process is a more circular journey, with four primary phases representing potential battlegrounds where marketers can win or lose: initial consideration; active evaluation, or the process of researching potential purchases; closure, when consumers buy brands; and post purchase, when consumers experience them. (McKinsey 2009)

Decision making process stage	Need identification	Information search	Evaluation of alternatives	Purchase	Post–purchase behaviour
Brand support	Creates brand awareness through an engaging, characterful brand image	Helps ensure that customer finds information about the brand	Creates a relevant brand promise, and brand image to assist the customer in choosing the brand	The purchase process makes it easy for the customer, maybe offering some reward for engagement	The brand provides a reminder to the customer
Suggested marketing activities	Develop an eye catching brand, with memorable brand elements. Put the brand in places the target audience will find it	Map the customer journey. Ensure that the brand is visible in the places that customers will search, and at all customer touchpoints.	Provide supporting evidence for the brand through all forms of marketing communication. Highlight its USP. Build its character. Give a strong call to action.	Make the purchase process straightforward. Offer an engagement reward. Ensure staff interactions create the start of a relationship.	Product labelling to put brand at forefront of customer's mind, email to stay in touch, give news, offer new products or services. Offer loyalty and advocacy rewards

Figure 2.1 How branding supports the customer through the decision-making process (adapted from Kotler and Armstrong (2010))

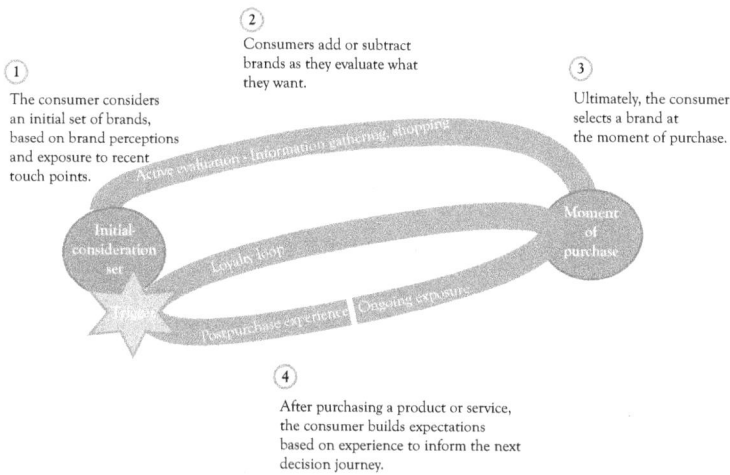

Figure 2.2 Four stage cyclical model of loyalty adapted from McKinsey

Loyalty in this model falls into two categories: active and passive.

Of consumers who profess loyalty to a brand, some are active loyalists, who not only stick with it but also recommend it. Others are passive loyalists who, whether from laziness or confusion caused by the dizzying array of choices, stay with a brand without being committed to it. (McKinsey 2009)

Importantly, they observe, passive loyalists are open to approaches from competitors. The key objective for a brand is to achieve what Kevin Roberts, CEO of Saatchi, identifies as a *lovemark*, which

draws on both high love and high respect. This is where enduring marriages and life-time love affairs belong, along with the places you really want to work, and the destinations in life that inspire and excite you. (Roberts 2017)

This loyalty loop essentially short circuits the decision-making process, with consumers opting for the brand with which they are most familiar, unless they have had cause for disappointment, so represents a major opportunity for establishing a relationship between the customer and organization.

Designing a Great Brand

The design of a great brand involves seven key aspects: purpose, consistency, emotion, flexibility, employee involvement, loyalty, and competitive awareness.

Unilever is committed to making sustainable living commonplace, and their logo is a visual expression of that commitment. Each icon has a rich meaning at its core and represents some aspect of their effort to make sustainable living commonplace: https://unilever.co.uk/about/who-we-are/our-logo/ (accessed February 2017).

The new Unilever logo and explanations on its website indicate the importance and an imaginative approach to embedding the values and characteristics of the brand in the logo. This is especially important when the brand has to support products in fields as diverse as tea and washing powders, as Unilever's does.

Unilever is committed to making sustainable living commonplace and our logo is a visual expression of that commitment. Each icon has a rich meaning at its core, and represents some aspect of our effort to make sustainable living commonplace.
https://www.unilever.co.uk/about/who-we-are/our-logo/(accessed Feb 2017)

Figure 2.3 The Unilever website explains all the icons that comprise the brand logo

How the Branding Theory can Support Development of a Powerful, Enduring Brand

Practitioners and academics alike have attempted to model how branding engages customers. This section uses just two of these, as the basis for a service excellence relationship; one from a renowned academic, Kevin Lane Keller, and one from Jean Noel Kapferer, the European authority on brands, and a practitioner or consultant. The models are selected because the Keller model concentrates on the customer relationship, while the Kapferer model focuses on building a brand that reflects the consumer back to himself or herself, and thereby establishes relevance and points upon which a relationship can be built.

If the brand is to truly attract, engage, and hold the customer over a lifetime, it needs to relate strongly to the target group, offering a strong bond through understanding and relevance. Expressing the brand values for all stakeholders, as Unilever has done, is an important element in building the trust that can form the basis for a lifetime relationship.

Keller's brand pyramid illustrates how this can work, starting with a recognition of shared values, building an understanding through a two-way conversation and knowledge, rising to the kind of intense active loyalty and advocacy that marks the brand as a *lovemark* (Roberts 2010).

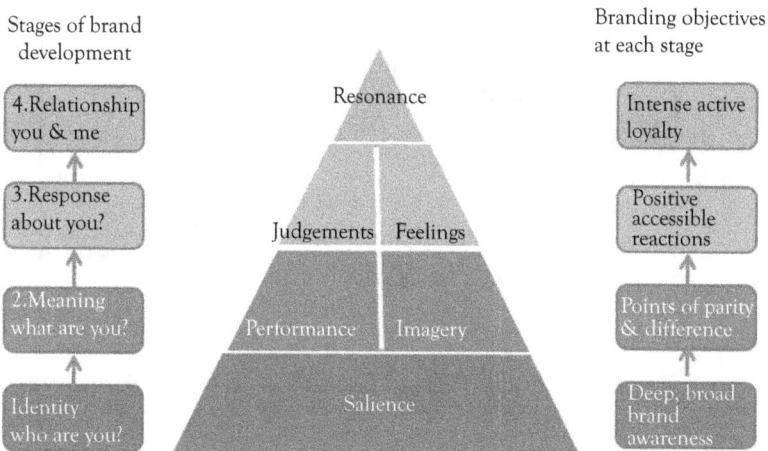

Figure 2.4 Keller's brand resonance pyramid, reproduced with kind permission of Pearson Publishers from Marketing Management (2nd edition) Kotler, Keller, Brady, Goodman

The following table shows how Mercedes Benz attempts to engage target customers in a deepening relationship through offering what they see as relevant benefits:

Kapferer adopts a different perspective from Keller and focuses attention on the two-way communications model, seeing brands as senders of information and consumers as receivers and vice versa. This encompasses the way in which branding and other forms of marketing communication are now augmented by social media activity.

Social media endows this model with greater power still, as consumers are not only connected to each other, but are hyper-linked to brands and any action that a brand takes has to accommodate speed and depth of responses from customers. Negative customer experiences left unmanaged can translate into a major communications problem. Savvy brands, however, have learned to cocreate with consumers on new products, communications, and ensure that any negative issues are effectively handled in real time.

Keller pyramid stages	How Mercedes Benz builds loyalty through the stages
1. Salience: who are you, Mercedes-Benz?	Mercedes-Benz is a premium luxury car manufacturer established since 1902. Its three-pointed star is recognizable anywhere. Is part of "German Big 3" along with Audi and BMW, the best-selling car manufacturers in the world.
2.Performance/Imagery: what are you, Mercedes-Benz? (cf. http://www.mercedes-benz.com/en/mercedes-benz/design/styling-a-masculine-edge/	Performance: Mercedes-Benz cars are renowned for their safety. Indeed, the German automaker innovated the crumple zone and was among the first to introduce the airbag and ABS systems. Able to create the most powerful engines thanks to its high performance division AMG (cf. CLA 45 AMG model). Cars are renowned for their comfortable and refined leather trims (cf. M-Class, C-Class, etc.) Imagery: Mercedes-Benz is known as a "masculine brand", notably through the design of its cars (horizontal lines) and don't hesitate to communicate about it). Elegance and excellence are also cultivated.
3. Judgments/Feelings: what do the customer think or feel about Mercedes-Benz?	Considering their features and history, Mercedes-Benz cars are judged prestigious and high quality. Imagery and all steps below arouse feelings such as sense of achievement, confidence or success.
4. Brand resonance: what about Mercedes-Benz and the customer?	Even if they are not purchasing a car, many people are attached to Mercedes-Benz through social media (17m likes on Facebook), clubs (Club Mercedes-Benz de France) and websites.

Figure 2.5 Application of the brand resonance pyramid to Mercedes Benz (adapted from https://bmvsmb.wordpress.com/2014/12/02/mercedes-benz-kellers-brand-resonance-pyramid/)

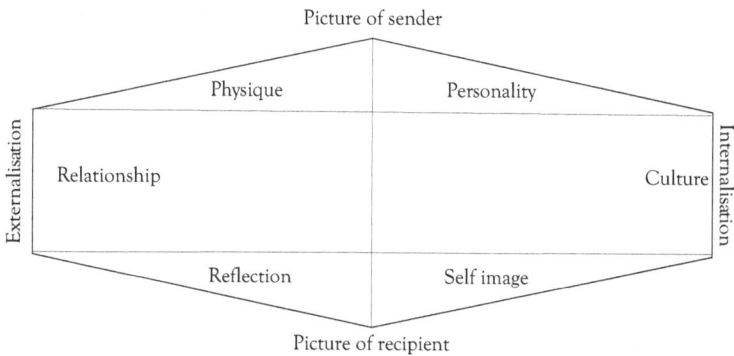

Figure 2.6 Kapferer's brand prism

Elements of the Brand Prism

Physique

Is the physical aspect of the brand including packaging, vehicle and staff livery, and brand web estate, and communities?

Personality

The brand's character, which forms the hook that attracts the selected target market, through projecting relevant values and characteristics. This needs to be managed across all touchpoints to show consistency, and in the digital world, has become at once more complex, and more important to manage. Customers build expectations of the brand from its personality, so brand actions need to be in keeping with its character, if customers are not to spot and comment on dissonance.

Culture

The system of values that the brand inherits from the company. Throughout the relationship a brand establishes with a customer, customers make subliminal judgments of the corporate values they perceive, and this reflects onto the brand, playing a part in repurchase and loyalty decisions.

Relationship

The relation between brand and consumer, and also between consumers, and how the brand facilitates this relationship. In this respect, the brand needs to be a leader within the community it creates, and creating a tribe is one of the fastest routes to advocacy. Digital word-of-mouth thrives in an active relationship where company and customer have different roles and can evolve in partnership.

Reflection (of the Consumer)

This is the stereotypical user of the brand. This is about the brand having a clear picture of their target market, maybe creating personas to facilitate that, identifying their demographics, psychographics, and shopping habits. This does not exclude others, but gives clarity for consumers. Brand advocates and bloggers can be valuable to promote the right image.

Self-Image

The mirror the target group holds up to itself. This is about how the customer wishes to be seen, what they want the world to see in them. This demands the brand appealing to the *higher self* of their consumers.

Action Points to Establish a Credible, Attractive Brand

1. Extend the brand universe to include all online properties.
2. Make sure brand personality is accurately reflected in all online interactions.
3. Let the real culture of the company do the talking.
4. Do not get between people, facilitate the interaction.
5. If 4 does not apply, then create as real an interaction as possible.
6. Talk to your ideal consumer—others will automatically connect to your ideal—use brand advocates, empower them, and let them speak for you.

Adapted from https://tuesdaydigital.wordpress.com/2013/01/06/applying-kapferers-brand-identity-model-to-digital-marketing/

Brand Names

Brand names fall into five types: descriptive, generic, arbitrary, suggestive, and fanciful.

Table 2.1 Different approaches to naming brands

Descriptive	Brand names suggest exactly what is being sold	Air France or Dunkin' Donuts are examples of descriptive brand names
Generic	Names identify an entire class of products or services; they are the weakest of all names because they offer no trademark protection. Nevertheless, they exist, increasingly in the online space: generic names often relate to low-cost products unsupported by advertising. Online, they represent an attempt to dominate an entire market segment. So, a generic name wins over distinctiveness. Some brand names started out as descriptive or suggestive, such as Hoover, which were adopted to describe a class of products and became generic by default (genericide).	Hotels.com, booking.com.
Arbitrary	Brand names are completely made-up names, which have no connection to the product or service.	Arbitrary brand names include Starbucks or Apple.
Suggestive	Names draw on metaphor and analogy to create positive associations. They are tougher to create and more challenging to market than descriptive names, but are more likely to be granted trademark protection and to become sustainable, scalable brands. Suggestive brand names give an idea of what the product or service is, but without being overtly descriptive. Many marketers consider suggestive brand names to be the best type of brand name.	Pinterest and YouTube. Greyhound for a bus company suggests the speed of racing dogs; Amazon for an online retailer suggests a mighty river of products.
Fanciful	Names are inventions, with no inherent meaning.	Kodak is the classic example: the name was constructed to offer symmetry and to have no meaning in any known language. Xerox has a real Greek root (xer-, meaning "dry," for the dry toner used in early copiers), but when it was first used, Xerox had no dictionary meaning.

Table 2.2 Examples of brand types

Descriptive	Acronym	Evocative
British Airways	KFC	Innocent
General Motors	IBM	Virgin Group
Dropbox	UPS	Nike
Parcelforce	DHL	Amazon
Experiential	**Geographical**	**Abstract**
AltaVista	New York Bagels, London	Alexa
HotBot	Transport, California Tan	Clusty
SideStep	London Transport, Champagne	Lycos
Kwikfit	Stilton Cheese	Etsy
Twitter	Newcastle Brown	Google

The name chosen should reinforce an important attribute or benefit association that forms its product positioning. For instance, PowerBook suggests not only the power of the machine itself, but offers a reflected glory for its owner (Apple Computer Inc.) too!

Brand Name Characteristics

1. **It should be distinctive**

   Your brand needs to stand out from the crowd and be memorable for your target market.

2. **It should promise**

   Your brand makes a promise of what the customer will receive following purchase of your product or service. This may be at any, or all of five levels, as shown in the following model: Your brand name and supporting symbol should indicate the level of quality customers can expect or may suggest superiority, tradition, or innovativeness, according to the nature of the desired target market.

3. **It should be appropriate**

   Many products or services aim to create a very definite image in the minds of the consumers. Silver Shadow is an appropriate brand name for a Rolls Royce car. Pocari Sweat works less well for a Japanese sports drink, especially in the global market.

4. **It should be easy to remember, pronounce, and spell**

   Kleenex, Nescafe, and Reebok are examples of such brand names. (Interestingly, these are all made-up names.)

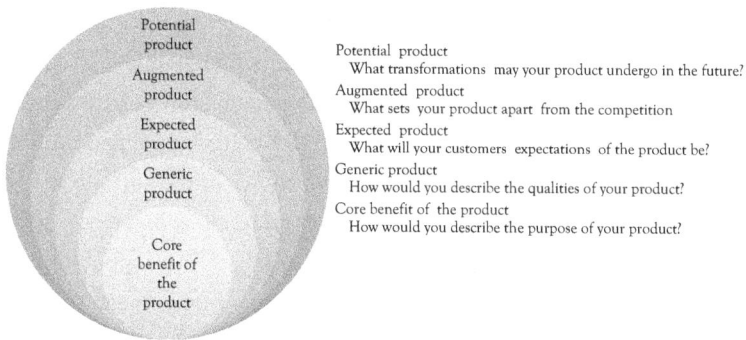

Potential product
What transformations may your product undergo in the future?
Augmented product
What sets your product apart from the competition
Expected product
What will your customers expectations of the product be?
Generic product
How would you describe the qualities of your product?
Core benefit of the product
How would you describe the purpose of your product?

Figure 2.7 *Five levels of product offering, Philip Kotler*
(https://brandeminence.wordpress.com/2014/01/15/256/)

5. **It should accommodate new products**

   National Cash Registers was a good brand name for cash registers, but when the company wanted to sell electronic point of sale terminals and computers, they contracted the name to its initials, NCR. Dunkin' Donuts is a good name for donuts, but would struggle to find relevance even in other food areas.

6. **It should be registerable and copyrightable in all target markets**

   It should work internationally. Jif cleaning products was forced to change to Cif when it entered Italy, as the Italian alphabet contains no letter J. Many are more unfortunate—Barf washing powder, sold in Iran, where it means *snow* would struggle to sell in English-speaking nations, the Vauxhall NOVA car translates into Spanish as No Va—it doesn't go!

   Your brand should also have *strategic relevance credibility within the audience availability uniqueness everyday functionality good gut feel.*

Brand Values

To me, marketing is about values. This is a very complicated world, it's a very noisy world. And we're not going to get the chance to get people to remember much about us. No company is. So we have to be really clear on what we want them to know about us.

—Steve Jobs, CEO Apple

Values lie at the very heart of your brand. From these, everything else radiates—physical appearance (design), the brand message (voice), and relationships (customer service). Brands that do not set out a clear picture of what their values are, may well acquire negative associations. So, creating a positive picture for the brand starts with determining the guiding values of the brand.

Core values define what an organization stands for, determining its culture and indicating an expected and set of behaviors. Organizational priorities and decisions, how a company spends its time and money, the kind of decisions it makes, all flow from its values. Customers, suppliers, and the business world understand the values an organization holds from seeing where it invests its resources, how its employees behave, rather than from its mission, or anything the company says. Prospective employees evaluate the company based on these things, and a strong set of core values, authentically expressed, can attract and retain talented employees, as well as reducing internal conflict, differentiating the brand, and attracting the desired customers. Values are woven tightly into the fabric of the company, are enduring, elemental, and actionable.

When core values are successfully used to develop an organization, they set the workplace culture and suggest how success is defined and

Table 2.3 Three approaches to brand values (http://cultbranding. com/ceo/core-values/)

IKEA's core values	Google's 10 things we know to be true	Southwest's *Live the Southwest Way*
1. Humbleness and willpower 2. Leadership by example 3. Daring to be different 4. Togetherness and enthusiasm 5. Cost-consciousness 6. Constant desire for renewal 7. Accept and delegate responsibility	1. Focus on the user and all else will follow 2. It is best to do one thing really, really well 3. Fast is better than slow 4. Democracy on the web works 5. You do not need to be at your desk to need an answer 6. You can make money without doing evil 7. There is always more information out there 8. The need for information crosses all borders 9. You can be serious without a suit 10. Great just is not good enough	1. Warrior Spirit (work hard; desire to the best; be courageous; display a sense of urgency; persevere; and innovate) 2. Servant's Heart (follow the golden rule; adhere to the basic principles; treat others with respect; put others first; be egalitarian; demonstrate proactive customer service; embrace the SWA family) 3. Fun-LUVing Attitude (have FUN; do not take yourself too seriously; maintain perspective (balance); celebrate successes; enjoy your work; be a passionate team player)

measured. As part of a branding exercise, congruence of the brand with the core values helps ensure that there is no dissonance for any of the stakeholder groups and gives authenticity to the brand.

Discovering Your Company's Core Values

Defining company values, working out how to express them, and how to keep them fresh are the foundation stones that promote a positive culture.

Lists of possible values abound, but using these can constrain what the team actually wants to stand for. An open brainstorm session with your employees is more likely to give a set of values that reflects who you are as a team and to be authentic. Authenticity of the brand has emerged as one of the most important aspects in establishing trust and credibility with consumers.

Brand Authenticity Definition

The extent to which consumers perceive a brand to be faithful toward itself, true to its consumers, motivated by caring and responsibility, and able to support consumers in being true to themselves.

Brand authenticity drives sales. Consumers use brands to minimize purchase risk, to express themselves, to manage our image, so in buying brands with authenticity, customers communicate personal authenticity.

Brand authenticity (perceived brand authenticity, PBA) comprises four key components:

Continuity (brand being faithful to itself)	Credibility (true to its consumers)
Integrity (motivated by caring and responsibility)	Symbolism (support consumers in being true to themselves)

Figure 2.8 Four dimensions of brand authenticity (Morhart et al. 2015)

Table 2.4 The top authentic brands adapted from https://marketing
*week.imgix.net/content/uploads/2014/09/Top_ranking_authentic_*
brands.jpg?auto=compress,format,&crop=faces,entropy,edges&fit=cro
p&q=60&w=460&h=

Rank	Mean authenticity score out of 10	Brand
1	7.9	Heinz
2	7.8	Disney
3	7.7	Ferrari
4	7.7	Google
5	7.6	Cadbury
6	7.6	Apple
7	7.4	VW
8	7.4	Microsoft
9	7.4	Landrover
10	7.4	Amazon

These four dimensions indicate that authenticity exceeds a simple *objective* attribute and has a psychological, subjective, and symbolic value as well—authentic brands are true to our personal values and help us be true to ourselves.

Making Core Values Stick

Studies show that values have to be internalized by employees and integrated into the culture, and crucially, to be reflected by the brand, for them to have a meaningful impact. Here are nine tips on making this happen:

Figure 2.9 Creating brand values Adapted from http://cultbranding.
com/ceo/core-values/

Brand values and the value of the brand are not synonymous, but a brand with a clear concept of its values will be perceived as authentic by its stakeholder groups and is likely to inspire loyalty and advocacy. This, in turn, will be reflected in higher profitability, and when a marketing audit is undertaken, there is a higher financial value for the brand.

Brand Backstory

Part of developing a relationship is to share your story; human beings all love a good story, and it can form an excellent starting point for a relationship. A backstory is a retrospective story that explains how different events combine in ways that make sense. Backstories are an especially strong narrative tool for any heritage brand because they create an opportunity to meld history with the future. A well-told backstory takes customers into the company's evolution to show how they developed into the brand they now are. It can also be an outstanding way of demonstrating values, such as hand crafting, using quality raw materials, partnership working, or employee ownership.

Using a backstory for brand identity means mapping the story through, based on real events, or a rose-tinted version of history. The brand shares aspects of its origins, funny events, and aspirations, over time, not necessarily in a timeline, to enhance consumers' understanding. Long-established Robson and Sons, based in Craster on the Northumberland coast, is a fourth-generation family business specializing in the traditional method of oak-smoking kippers and salmon. Its website celebrates the quality of its source ingredients, the history of their production techniques, and their development, all against a sepia-tinted fade-out photograph of Craster village. Video clips engage the customer by showing the sea, harbor, and boats, as well as production techniques, old and new. This discussion also covers the importance of selecting only top-quality fish.

Clearly, using an authentic backstory is ideal, but many new brands build a backstory from scratch, choosing a starting point and developing from there, adding anecdotes and characters to create interest. This may involve *borrowing*, adapting, or copying a successful backstory from another company, or history or mythology. Derwent Valley Foods famously adopted Phileas Fogg, the protagonist in the 1873, Jules Verne

> Built in 1856 by the Craster family, "Robsons Smokehouse" is now the only smokehouse in Craster.
>
> James William Robson moved to Craster around 1890, arriving in Craster from a herring yard in Newton. He later bought the smokehouse from the Craster family and the business was born in 1906.
>
> From then "Robsons Smokehouse" passed through four generations and today is run by Neil Robson. His father Alan, still keeps a keen eye on the business and visits the smokehouse every day.
>
> The traditional methods of smoking are still used today and the tradition has been passed on to yet another generation. Neil's daughter, Olivia, is as passionate about the tradition as her father, grandfather and great grandfather before her.

Figure 2.10 Robson and Sons backstory (http://kipper.co.uk, L. Robson and Sons Ltd.)

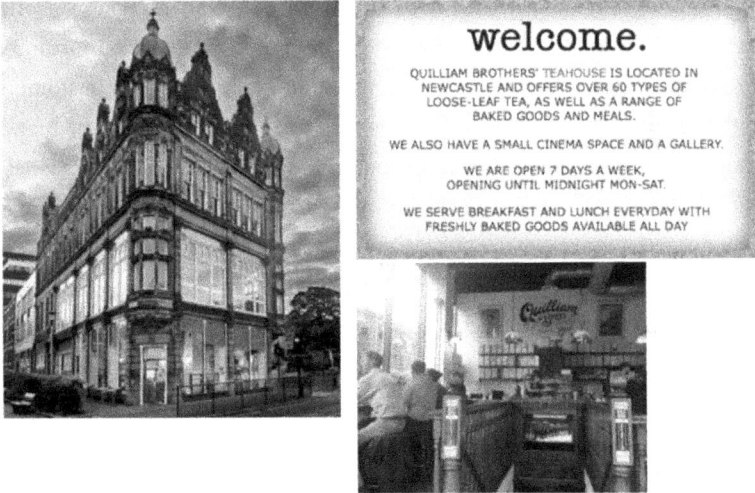

welcome.

QUILLIAM BROTHERS' TEAHOUSE IS LOCATED IN NEWCASTLE AND OFFERS OVER 60 TYPES OF LOOSE-LEAF TEA, AS WELL AS A RANGE OF BAKED GOODS AND MEALS.

WE ALSO HAVE A SMALL CINEMA SPACE AND A GALLERY.

WE ARE OPEN 7 DAYS A WEEK, OPENING UNTIL MIDNIGHT MON-SAT.

WE SERVE BREAKFAST AND LUNCH EVERYDAY WITH FRESHLY BAKED GOODS AVAILABLE ALL DAY

Figure 2.11 Quilliam Brothers shop exterior and interior and website excerpt Quilliam brothers Tea rooms, Newcastle upon Tyne

Table 2.5 Points to start a backstory adapted from (http://thestoryof telling.com/what-is-a-brand-story/)

Truth	Purpose	Vision	Values
Products and services	Your people	Value you deliver	Name & Tagline
Content & Copy	Design	Your actions	Customer experience
Price & Quality	Position & Perception	Distribution	Location
Ubiquity or Scarcity	Community	Reputation	Reaction & Reach

Table 2.6 Tom's Shoes website showing their brand differentiation on CSR (http://toms.com)

Tom's Shoes original commitment	Tom's Shoes recent commitment

Table 2.7 Ten tips to use your backstory to build brand equity adapted from (https://brandingstrategyinsider.com/2016/09/how-to-build-a-strong-brand-backstory.html#.WLGEnnecau4)

1.	How did you get to where you are now—where did your brand start, doing what, with how many people?
2.	What happened along the way that was exciting, weird, fun, challenging, and extraordinary?
3.	Who were the main characters—what did they bring to the brand, and what did they fail to see? Who proved to be the heroes and the villains?
4.	When did things look impossible—what nearly killed the company, and what happened to save the brand?
5.	Who made the (many) decisions that changed your brand over the years, and what were the circumstances?
6.	Why was that important—if the decision was acted on? Where might that have led if others had agreed (good or bad)?
7.	What are some of the side-stories around what your brand is famous for that you can reveal (and were never able to before)?
8.	Which other well-known people or events has the brand been involved with in the course of its history? What was the nature of the brand's involvement?
9.	How did your journey make you the brand you are?
10.	What signs of your backstory are visible (even celebrated) in your brand today?

novel, *Around the World in Eighty Days,* as their brand hero, who traveled the world and returned to make snacks in Medomsley Road, Consett. Another example of this is the highly successful Quilliam Brothers' tea rooms in Newcastle, which has been operating for only a few years, and yet presents a well-developed history, both in reality and on their website. They have incorporated some of their personal passions for grass root arts and excellent tea and cakes into their Budapest-style tea house.

The aforementioned points all form important starting points for a backstory, and any of them can be a route in to this valuable brand asset. For real excellence, the backstory needs to be not only engaging, but authentic, and therefore, true; so, if you do not have the history, make another story, like Tom's Shoes, which started by giving a pair of shoes for a child in poverty for every pair bought by a customer and has now moved into other areas of philanthropy.

Mapping the Customer Journey

Mapping the customer journey for all interactions with the brand enables a stronger understanding of what the customer experiences, as well as gaining a better appreciation of their responses at each stage, and can encourage the passion required for active loyalty and advocacy. For the business, these intense relationships are important, as research suggests that the costs of acquiring new customers can be as much as five times that of servicing existing customers, so they deliver a higher profit margin. Frederick Reicheld of Bain and Company (the inventor of the NetPromoter) found that increasing customer retention rates by 5 percent increases profits by 25 percent to 95 percent.

The McKinsey team suggest that, for a business to increase the

percentage of active loyalists requires not only integrating customer-facing activities into the marketing organization but also subtler forms of organizational cooperation. These include identifying active loyalists through customer research, as well as understanding what drives that loyalty and how to harness it with word-of-mouth programs. Companies need an integrated, organization-wide 'voice of the customer,' with skills from advertising to public relations, product development, market research, and data management. (McKinsey 2009)

Table 2.8 Two-thirds of the touchpoints during the active-evaluation phase involve consumer-driven activities such as Internet reviews and word-of-mouth recommendations from friends and family

Most influential touch points by stage of consumer decision % effectiveness	Initial consideration set	Active evaluation	Closure
Store/Agent/dealer interactions	12	26	42
Consumer driven marketing- Word of mouth online research Off-line reviews	21	37	31
Past experience	28	10	5
Company driven marketing- Traditional advertising Direct marketing Sponsorship in-store product experience Salesperson contact	39	26	22

The preceding figure suggests that establishing such commitment demands active involvement from the customer, hence the requests for customers to blog, vlog, and introduce friends to brands, as well as provide service feedback via Feefo, NetPromoter, Customersure, and SurveyMonkey.

To connect with customers at each touchpoint requires the brand to establish a set of clearly recognizable attributes or elements to ensure that each contact reinforces the brand message.

Brand Elements

A brand comprises many diverse features that make a connection and a communication with a consumer. These include tangible elements that create your brand identity through sensory cues, such as visual, auditory, and olfactory. The following image shows examples for a range of brand elements, drawn on some of the best known brands:

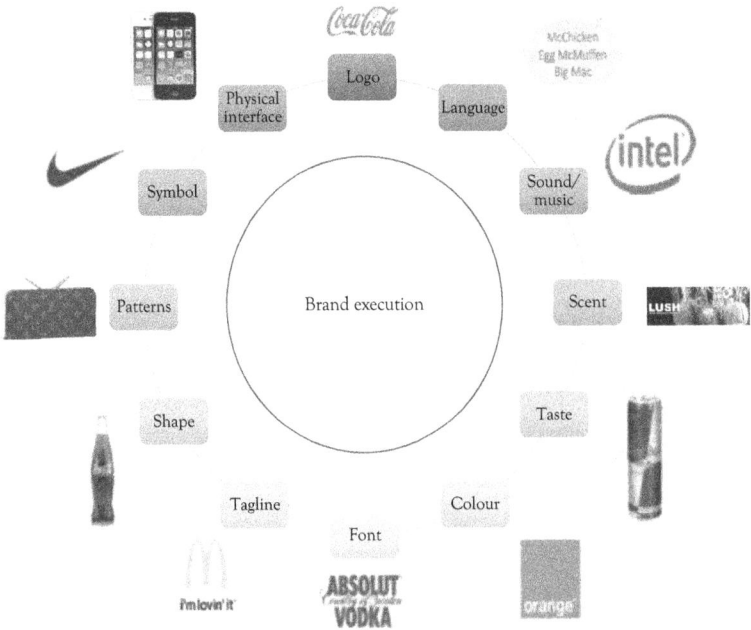

Figure 2.12 Brand elements adapted from (http://thehealthcompass. org/how-to-guides/how-create-brand-strategy-part-3-developing-personality-and-look-brand)

Branding guru Kevin Lane Keller cites six criteria for brand elements, which fall into two groups with either an offensive or defensive role. Differing strengths and weaknesses accrue to each brand element. Building brand equity demands establishing a balance between the different elements in their verbal and visual context to maximize their collective contribution (Keller 2006, p. 178).

Key Criteria for Brand Elements

Brand Association

Brand association is anything that is deep seated in customer's mind about the brand. Brand owners seek positive associations that will create a *halo effect* for the brand, so customers perceive the brand in

Table 2.9 Key criteria for brand elements (Keller 2006, p. 178)

Offensive role	Defensive role
1. Memorability	4. Transferability
2. Meaningfulness	5. Adaptability
3. Likability	6. Protectability

Table 2.10 Brand elements

	Brand elements				
Criterion	Brand names and URL's	Logos and symbols	Characters	Slogans and jingles	Packaging and signage
Memorability	Can be chosen to enhance brand recall and recognition	Generally more useful for brand recognition	Generally more useful for brand recognition	Can be chosen to enhance brand recall and recognition	Generally more useful for brand recognition
Meaningfulness	Can reinforce almost any type of association, although sometimes only indirect	Can reinforce almost any type of association, although sometimes only indirect	Generally more useful for non product related imagery and brand personality	Can convey almost any type of association explicitly	Can convey almost any type of association explicitly
Likability	Can evoke much verbal imagery	Can provoke visual appeal	Can generate human qualities	Can evoke much verbal imagery	Can combine visual and verbal appeal
Transferability	Can be somewhat limited	Excellent	Can be somewhat limited	Can be somewhat limited	Good
Adaptability	Difficult	Can typically be redesigned	Can typically be redesigned	Can be modified	Can typically be redesigned
Protectability	Generally good, but with limits	Excellent	Excellent	Excellent	Can be closely copied

Source: Adapted from http://van-haaften.nl/branding/corporate-branding/77-brand-elements

a positive light. Brand associations are top of consumers' minds when the brand is talked about. They link with the implicit and explicit meanings that a consumer relates or associates with a specific brand name. Brand association can also be defined as the degree to which a specific product or service is recognized within its product, service class, or category.

Brand associations are formed on the following basis:

1. Customers contact with the organization and its employees
2. Advertisements
3. Word-of-mouth publicity
4. Price at which the brand is sold
5. Celebrity or big entity association
6. Quality of the product
7. Products and schemes offered by competitors
8. Product class or category to which the brand belongs
9. POP (point of purchase) displays, and so on

Positive brand associations are developed if the product that the brand depicts is durable, marketable, and desirable. Customers must be convinced that the brand possesses the features and attributes satisfying their needs, giving them a positive impression about the product. Positive brand association helps an organization to gain goodwill and obstructs competitor entry into the market.

Brand Equity Definition

Brand equity refers to a value premium that a company generates from a product with a recognizable name, when compared with a generic equivalent. Companies can create brand equity for their products by making them memorable, easily recognizable, and superior in quality and reliability. Mass marketing campaigns also help to create brand equity (http://investopedia.com/terms/b/brandequity.asp#ixzz4ZizT3y00).

Brand equity is the value of the brand from the consumer perspective, encompassing all the positives and negatives associated with the brand, built up over time, and exposure to the brand. The perception of the brand will differ for different groups of customer, according to its relevance to them. A set of positive associations and a favorable perception can be reflected as a significant brand equity (or value).

Positive brand equity can turn into either tangible or intangible value. Positive brand equity produces increases in revenue or profits, while intangible value manifests as awareness or goodwill. If a company has a major product recall or experiences a widely publicized environmental disaster, the brand is likely to develop negative brand equity.

Brand equity is important when a company wants to expand its product line. Positive equity increases the likelihood of customers buying the new product by linking it with a familiar, successful brand. Family branding companies, such as Heinz and Cadbury, who market many products under the same brand name depend on this. This approach works well, unless there is a major catastrophe for the parent brand.

Brand equity is a weather vane for company strength and performance, specifically in the stock markets, and brands are given a value in the balance sheet. Most literature focuses on the financial value of brands when there is no change of ownership. Often, acquisitions are undertaken purely because the new owner perceives an opportunity to augment the brand equity through new marketing. This was the case when Hammerite paint, first developed in 1962 by Finnigan's Northumberland factory, was acquired in the 1980s by Hunting plc. who later sold to Williams Holdings in 1993. ICI acquired the company from Williams Holdings in 1998 for the value of the Hammerite paint brand, which they have successfully grown. Companies in the same industry often compete on brand equity as the precursor to building market share.

Figure 2.13 Heinz family branded products. Taken from http://heinz. co.uk/products

Employer Branding

If the brand is a hook for customers, then that applies equally to employees and potential employees. If the organization does things that make employees feel valued, they spread positive word-of-mouth, and in the same way that customers are drawn to the organization and build trust in it, so too will staff.

Staff are the means by which service is given to customers, especially in very high-touch organizations, with a lot of staff customer interaction. Recruiting staff whose values chime with the brand will help embed the brand values, and employer branding is the key tool in ensuring that the right kind of staff are attracted to the organization in the first place. It is easier to train people in the required skills than it is to train the correct attitude, so the mantra is *Recruit for attitude rather than skills*. In a marketplace such as retail, where hidden services, such as daily contact and communication for people who may be isolated due to age, disability, ethnicity, and other factors, having empathetic staff is increasingly important.

The ability to attract and recruit the best staff may well give an organization a competitive edge against its competitors. It is becoming an area of increasing concern, despite high unemployment statistics. "In 2014, 36 percent of global employers reported talent shortages, the highest percentage since 2007, and in a more recent 2015 survey, 73 percent of CEOs reported being concerned about the availability of key skills" (https://hbr.org/2015/05/ceos-need-to-pay-attention-to-employer-branding).

The concept was coined in the mid-1990s, describing an organization's employer reputation distinct from its more general brand reputation. Creation of a strong employer brand assumed importance in the early 2000s, when companies like Unilever, Shell, and P&G began to view their employer branding as equal to their consumer branding. Now, most major organizations offer an employee value proposition, defining the key benefits offered by the company as an employer, and employer brand guidelines for use in advertising and internal marketing.

All organizations have, consciously or otherwise, an employer brand. It is the way in which organizations differentiate themselves in the labor market, enabling them to recruit, retain, and engage the right people. A strong employer brand helps businesses compete for the best talent and establish credibility. It should connect with an organization's values

| Secure our long-term recruitment needs | Build our employer brand on a global level | Differentiate ourselves from competitors | Build our employer brand on a local level |

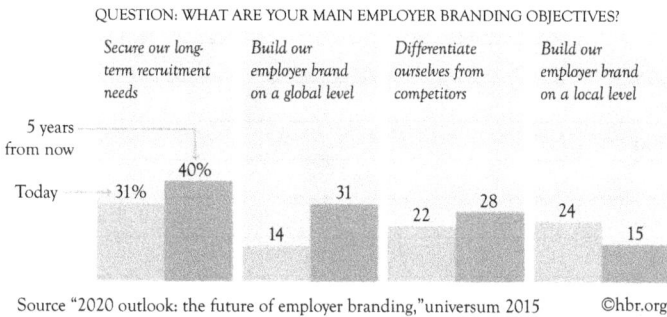

Source "2020 outlook: the future of employer branding,"universum 2015   ©hbr.org

Figure 2.14 Growing strategic importance of the employer brand: what CEOs expect it to do for the company by 2020 reproduced with kind permission of Harvard Business Review

and must run consistently through its approach to people management (Chartered Institute of Personnel And Development: https://cipd.co.uk/knowledge/fundamentals/people/recruitment/brand-factsheet#).

Employer branding is gaining in importance, as shown by the above chart; exactly as with consumers, it offers differentiation and a robust long-term strategy, giving sustainable recruitment into the future and across geographical divides:

So strong has employer branding become that there is now an organization, Universum, that is a global leader in employer branding. They work with top universities, alumni groups, and professional organizations to gather insights from students and professionals in 60 countries in order to advice employers on how to attract and retain talent that fits their culture and purpose (http://universumglobal.com).

Enhancing the Employer Brand

Given the strategic importance of the employer brand, strategic design is important, and the following table overleaf indicates an approach to strengthening the employer brand perception.

1. Evaluate your current employer brand awareness and reputation, through survey research among your key external target audiences
2. Define how you would like to be seen as an employer based on a realistic assessment of your distinctive strengths and translate this into a clear and compelling employee value proposition

Students
Engineering/IT
Google
Microsoft
Apple
Business
Google
Apple
EY (Ernst & Young)

Figure 2.15 Top employer brands 2016, seen from a student and a business perspective adapted from Universum

3. Be more proactive in using social media to share inside stories that highlight your strengths and build a more authentic and engaging employer brand reputation

4. Ensure that every function within the organization understands the value of a strong employer brand to the success of the business and the role they need to play in sustaining a consistent brand experience and reputation

5. Ensure you have a LinkedIn company page that gives a strong flavor of what you do and shows a united company by branding pictures, using the company logo, and so on

6. Measure your talent brand index on LinkedIn

7. Have a strong social media presence boosted by inputs from staff at all levels

8. encourage staff to share the projects they are engaged in, fun they are having etc

Adapted from https://hbr.org/2015/05/ceos-need-to-pay-attention-to-employer-branding

Refreshing the Brand

As a business grows and evolves, the brand needs to adapt to represent the current vision and mission of the company. Brands also need to meet emerging needs of customers, trends, and other changes in the marketplace.

Microsoft	1. Microsoft's employer branding strategy starts with their Careers site, which gives job openings, a Jobs blog and a bit of 'life at Microsoft,' detailing the company's values and career development opportunities.
	2. Microsoft's online presence extends to Twitter, Facebook and LinkedIn to engage with potential employees across all major social networks.
	3. There is a separate Facebook page for 'Women at Microsoft,' almost as popular as their primary careers page and is a unique insight into the women working at the company.
	4. The Microsoft Careers Youtube channel has over 100 videos, including a 'Day in the Life' series where potential employees can see many aspects of working for Microsoft and hear the opinions of program managers and developers.
Google	1. Google regularly tops the Employers survey by Universum and their global reputation as a great place to work is behind their success.
	2. Life at Google G+ page has more than 2.2m followers, which it updates with information about the unique events that they hold for their employees such as their Googleween Halloween event.
	3. Googles 'work hard, play hard' values are well known by the public through continually updating the internet about the employee perks (such as nap pods and free meals).
	4. Combined with their careers tagline of 'Do cool things that matter,' Google promotes an enjoyable environment to work in.
	5. Google has also shown that they care about the wellbeing of their staff by conducting their own study, gDNA to learn how their employees balance work life and personal life.
pwc	1. Price Waterhouse Coopers has a dedicated twitter account for their UK Careers which keeps potential talent updated on PwC news and what it is like to work for the multinational organisation.
	2. They also use Twitter to promote various unique insights into the organisation, including live web chats with current employees and apprentices that provide interested candidates with the opportunity to ask questions about the office environment.
	3. The company's career website also incorporates a 'People's blog' where posts are written by employees that describe their experiences of working for PwC. If you like what you see, we are currently listing 5 PwC Job vacancies, including roles in Data Analytics and einvestigations.

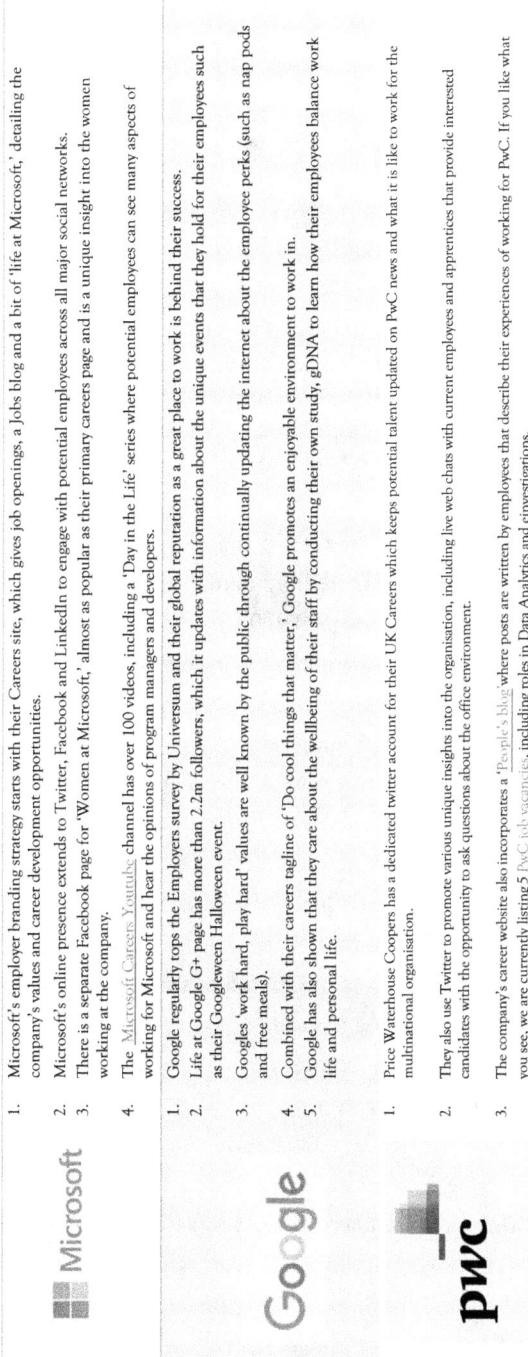

Figure 2.16 Three top employer brands 2016

Adapted from *http://uk.dice.com/technews/top-3-examples-of-positive-employer-branding/*

Microsoft has changed its image over the years, while maintaining its core value, its brand has to evolve to stay as a market leader and embody current trends. A fresh brand will reflect a current and up-to-date image of a company. This is reassuring to its existing customers and attractive to new ones. Here you can see the evolution of the Microsoft logo:

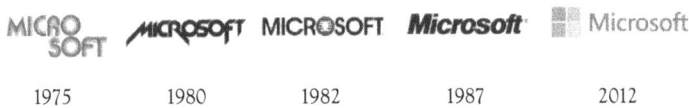

| 1975 | 1980 | 1982 | 1987 | 2012 |

Figure 2.17 Evolution of the Microsoft brand reproduced with kind permission from(https://google.co.uk/search?q=evolution+of+the+Mic rosoft+logo.&client=safari&rls=en&tbm=isch&tbo=u&source=univ& sa=X&ved=0ahUKEwjekv3_0LjSAhVFGsAKHdjHAD8Q7AkIKA& biw=1199&bih=744#imgrc=KGuMHnJAjDJbBM)

If Microsoft had retained their 1975 branding today against Apple's current brand, it would look incredibly dated. The logo has evolved to reflect the current trends from the 1970's *psychedelic* logo to the slick, simplistic, and functional logo we currently recognize.

Without evolution, the brand loses its edge against its competitors and its relevance with the target audience.

Apple's first personal computers were aimed at specialists and technically savvy individuals who *knew what they were doing* in the computer world. As the technology became more accessible, so did their products, and in turn, their target audience grew massively. Apple began to promote their stylish, user-friendly products with a stylish, user-friendly brand. This repositioning came with a brand refresh to set Apple aside from their rival competitors Microsoft. As a result, Apple is consistently at the top of the Coolbrands (http://coolbrands.uk.com) list and has achieved the accolade of becoming a *lovemark*.

A name change, a merger, or a separation can be signified by a brand change, but remaining recognizable and maintaining the trust and loyalty established with your audience is vital. When Lloyds and TSB split, Lloyds had to rebrand. By retaining the recognizable element of the brand (the black horse) and adding new, crisp typography, the newly formed Lloyds bank is still reputable on the high street, while its refreshed image assures their customers that change can be a positive thing.

Figure 2.18 Evolution of the Apple brand reproduced with kind permission of Clarity Quest Marketing

End of Chapter Summary

The chapter has explored, firstly, the role of the brand throughout the customer decision-making process. It has explained the way in which equity and value is built by creating a strong, authentic brand that has personality and expresses clear values and principles.

The naming and strategy behind successful branding are covered and the need to do this in line with overall corporate strategy.

Brand elements and the story behind the brand are investigated as key means of attracting potential customers through creating a likeable personality for the brand to begin its relationship with customers and potential recruits.

Branding also needs to be seen from the perspective of employees and prospective recruits to the organization. Although often overlooked, people employed by the organization are a key element of the extended marketing mix, and therefore, recruitment needs to reflect this. Finally, the need for brand refreshment in a highly dynamic and competitive environment is covered.

Key Terms

Customer touchpoint—every aspect of the organization that a customer encounters—*before, during, or after they purchase something from you.* A website, physical presence.

Finding Your Customer Touchpoints

Identify your customer touchpoints by making a list of all the places and times your customers might come into contact with your brand.

Table 2.11 Shifts in brand preferences based on Coolbrands (http://s3.coolbrands.uk.com/files/2013/09/CB-2013-14-Official-Results-68p914.pdf)

2011	2012	2013	2014	2015	2016
Aston Martin	Apple	Apple	Apple	Apple	Apple
Apple	YouTube	Aston Martin	Samsung	Aston Martin Nike	Google
Rolex	Aston Martin	Rolex	Google Microsoft	CHANEL Glastonbury	Samsung
Bang and Olufsen	Twitter	Nike	Verizon	Google YouTube	Amazon
BlackBerry	Google	Glastonbury Festival	GE	Dom Pérignon Rolex	Microsoft
Google	BBC iPlayer	YouTube	AT&T	Netflix	Verizon
Ferrari	Virgin	Google	Amazon	Bang & Olufsen	AT&T
Nike	Bang and Olufsen	Twitter	Walmart		Walmart
YouTube	Liberty	Virgin Atlantic	IBM		China Mobile
Alexander McQueen	Sony	Ray-Ban	Toyota		Wells Fargo
					Toyota McDonalds
					GE
					China Construction

This list makes a good starting point, but every business is different, so touchpoints need to be identified. Added to that, each touchpoint can have layers. *Communication* could encompass touchpoints across many channels, while a brick-and-mortar store needs touchpoints signage to help people locate it, directions to the car park, and the diverse departments inside the store.

Extended marketing mix: the marketing mix is seen as the key elements required to achieve successful sales of product. For the marketing of physical products: this was identified as product, price, place, and promotion. As services have become more important to world economies, and the differences in marketing these have been recognized, basic product mix has been extended to include people, physical evidence, and process. A further element, productivity and quality, is also sometimes included, but for service excellence, philosophy holds equal importance to the other elements, so for services, a nine Ps version holds greater validity.

Table 2.12 What the world's best business leaders say about brands (https://addicted2success.com/quotes/9-killer-branding-quotes-from-the-worlds-top-billionaires/)

"Make every detail perfect, and limit the number of details to perfect." Jack Dorsey	"Too many companies want their brands to reflect some idealised, perfected image of themselves. As a consequence, their brands acquire no texture, no character." Richard Branson
"Design is not just what it looks like and feels like. Design is how it works." Steve Jobs	"Your premium brand had better be delivering something special, or it's not going to get the business." Warren Buffett

Table 2.13 Customer touchpoints (https://surveymonkey.co.uk/mp/identify-customer-touchpoints/)

Before purchase	During purchase	After purchase
Social media	Store or office	Billing
Ratings and reviews	Website	Transactional emails
Testimonials	Catalog	Marketing emails
Word-of-mouth	Promotions	Service and support teams
Community involvement	Staff or sales team	Online help center
Advertising	Phone system	Follow-ups
Marketing or PR	Point of sale	Thank you cards

Figure 2.19 Extended marketing mix

End of Chapter Review Questions

Does your organization's branding reinforce excellence? High or Low					
How much does your brand say about excellence?					
How much does your brand convey trust?					

Does your brand have personality?		
Does your organization have a real individual or group of people for customers to associate with?	Yes	No
Does your organization have a credible back story that people can understand, connect with, and talk about?	Yes	No
Do you have a way to recognize your customers by name, face, or voice so that they are not treated like new customers every time they come to you?	Yes	No
Can individual employees choose to bend or change policies based on their interactions with customers?	Yes	No
If you read your marketing sales or web literature out loud, does it sound as though a real person is saying it?	Yes	No
Are individual employees encouraged to tell friends, families, and contacts about what they do, and are they given training in how the company describes and positions itself?	Yes	No

How likeable is your brand?					
Does your brand have something different from other brands?					
Does your brand have a twist to it? How does the brand work outside the region?					
Is your brand worth talking about, or does it have a viral aspect to it?					
Is your brand significant, honest, and does it have depth and soul?					
Does the brand fit with the organization, or you?					
Does the brand reflect the values of customers, staff?					
Does the brand foster individuals rather than people?					
Does the brand convey a passion, loyalty, and a deep belief in itself?					
Does your brand have a creditable heritage?					
Does the brand have a shareable hook? Does the brand offer something of value? Does the brand have motives beyond profit?					

Adapted from *Personality Not included*: Rohit Bharagava McGraw Hill 2008.

How strong is your employer brand?					
How high is your current employer brand awareness and reputation?					
Do you have a clear and compelling employee value proposition?					
Do you have a strong online presence, employing all the key social media platforms?					
Do you share inside stories that highlight your strengths and build a more authentic and engaging employer brand reputation?					
Does every function within the organization understand the value of a strong employer brand to the success of the business?					
Do staff appreciate the role they need to play in sustaining a consistent brand experience and reputation?					
Do you have a detailed LinkedIn page giving a good flavor of your organization and presenting your employee value proposition?					
Do all staff have a corporate look to their profile, reflecting a cohesive approach?					
Is everyone at all levels involved in maintaining your social media presence?					
Do staff write about their experiences, sharing news about the company to amplify the brand and accelerate the network effect?					
Do staff write-ups sound authentic, and are they written by real staff, not marketing people?					

Do you give potential staff real insights into what you offer?						
Do you measure your talent brand index on LinkedIn?						
Do you actively work to raise your talent brand index?						

Based on https://hbr.org/2015/05/ceos-need-to-pay-attention-to-employer-branding

References

Kotler, P., and G. Armstrong. 2010. *Principles of Marketing*, 13th ed. Prentice Hall.

https://surveymonkey.co.uk/mp/identify-customer-touchpoints/

https://reference.com/business-finance/examples-brand-names-4cadf3 91d2ebdee2

http://mckinsey.com/business-functions/marketing-and-sales/our-insights/the-consumer-decision-journey

https://blog.hubspot.com/blog/tabid/6307/bid/31739/7-Components-That-Comprise-a-Comprehensive-Brand-Strategy.aspx#sm.00002mh txz1czff73sm9gs4p8e30c

http://investopedia.com/terms/b/brandequity.asp

http://saatchikevin.com/lovemarks/future-beyond-brands/

https://hbr.org/2015/05/ceos-need-to-pay-attention-to-employer-branding

https://hbr.org/2014/10/the-value-of-keeping-the-right-customers

https://digitalintelligencetoday.com/new-brand-authenticity-scale-released-how-authentic-are-you/

https://sciencedirect.com/science/article/pii/S1057740814001089

CHAPTER 3

Ensure Quality

Chapter Objectives

- To outline how quality of both the product and service helps deliver customer satisfaction and meet the promise of the brand.
- To offer frameworks for understanding perceptions of quality from both customer and company perspectives.
- To suggest ways of enhancing product and service quality in ways that are meaningful to customers and potential customers.
- To understand the role that quality plays in supporting brand development.
- To offer suggestions for using quality as part of the marketing message.

Chapter Profile

Customers have been attracted to the organization by the brand that represents it; their continued custom depends on the level of satisfaction that they experience in their interactions with the organization. They will be looking for the brand promise to be delivered through product quality, supported by matching service, both giving a consistent message. Quality of service, even in a product-driven market, is often one of the key differentiators between providers from a customer perspective.

Key questions to address are:

- How can you get the promise right and deliver what and when you say?
- Is quality important to your customers, and how do you measure it versus how your customers measure it?

- How to evaluate different aspects of quality or TQM?
- Why is it important to embed excellence and quality within the team?
- Different quality measures: why measure quality?
- Recruitment and training to ensure quality and excellence.
- Values—add in—ensure they are important to your customer; do they stand the "SO WHAT" test?
- Process/staff/standards and so on—rights and responsibilities, empowerment.
- Quality is in the eye of the beholder—changes over time; how can you keep it fresh? Price versus quality, inequalities.

Key Terms

Customer Touchpoint

Customer touchpoints are all of the points within a customer journey that the customer encounters your brand. Often when businesses are mapping touchpoints, they look at it from their perspective, rather than from the customer perspective. They are a valuable tool when viewed as a whole experience and as individual opportunities to improve the customer experience.

Moments of Truth

Any instance of contact or interaction between a customer and an organization (through a product, sales force, or visit) that gives the customer an opportunity to form (or change) an impression about the organization.

Value for Money

A sum of all benefits derived from every purchase or every sum of money spent. Value for money is based not only on the minimum purchase price (economy), but also on the maximum efficiency and effectiveness of the purchase, so involves all free gifts, service, brand associations, and so on.

Definition: Service Quality

An assessment of how well a delivered *service* conforms to the client's expectations. *Service* business operators often assess the *service quality* provided to their customers in order to improve their *service*, to quickly identify problems, and to better assess client satisfaction. http://business-dictionary.com/definition/service-quality.html

Such is the importance of service quality that definitions abound: Lehtinen (1983) defines service quality in terms of corporate image, quality, interactive quality, and physical quality. Gronroos (1983) distinguishes *what* is delivered—*technical quality* from *how* it is delivered—*functional quality*. The most definitive comes from Parasuraman et al. (1991), which view service quality as an attitude, linked but not equal to satisfaction, based on the customer's perception of service in relation to their expectations of service.

Why Quality Matters

Research suggests that mistakes and inefficiencies can account for up to 40 per cent of the operating costs in a service organization. Minimizing this waste and meeting customer expectations are the major challenges facing service managers, so quality improvement is paramount for service organizations. This cost does not include the loss of dissatisfied customers.

Customer service and people development programs significantly enhance organizational results, indicating a high correlation between service quality and profitability. Research done by Sears found that a "five percent gain in employee satisfaction drives a one percent gain in customer satisfaction which, in turn, leads to an additional 0.5 percent increase in profit." Similarly, the Canadian Imperial Bank of Commerce used the service–profitability cycle to show that each percentage increase in customer loyalty generates an additional percent in the net profit.

Sustained profitability, efficient resource utilization, higher levels of customer/client/user satisfaction, all produce a great reputation that further builds public confidence. Contrary to expectations, this proves a *right first-time service* enables costs to fall, rather than rise. Coupled with the reduction in waste is the saving from service staff having to put wrongs right. Right first time has a cost, but when that fails, time

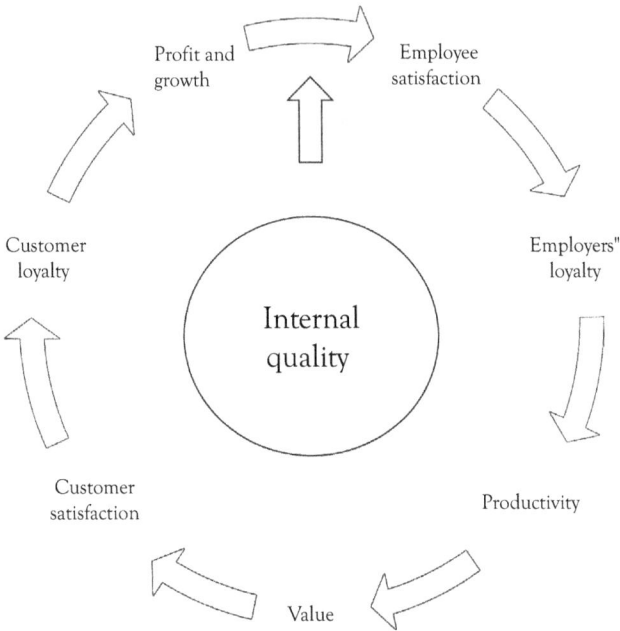

Figure 3.1 Service profit chain (Heskett et al. 1997)

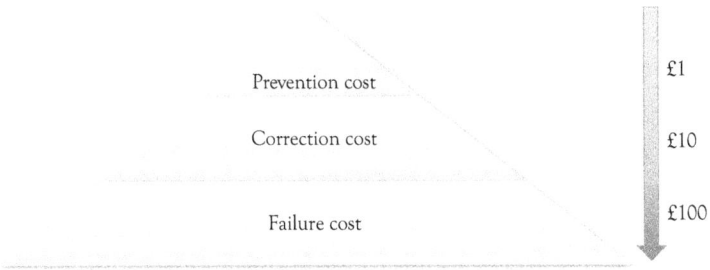

Figure 3.2 The 1:10:100 rule

and compensation to put it right incurs a cost estimated at 10 times the original, and this escalates further when the problem is not dealt with promptly. The 1:10:100 rule explains how failure to address one cost escalates the loss in terms of dollars. Costs of poor quality include: (1) prevention, (2) appraisal, (3) internal failure, and (4) external failure. Prevention cost should take priority because it is much less costly to prevent a defect than to correct one.

Consistently good quality service is one of the key factors in building loyalty, and customers' loyalty increases profits generated by the company. Reliable service helps customers to be lenient, in the event that there is an error, customers are likely to overlook it, rather than switch to competitors at the first mistake. Service is the main element in customers electing to join rival companies, accounting for 69 percent cases of defection. By contrast, low product quality causes only 13 percent of defections.

Poor service can produce:

- Lost profit from abandoned transaction
- Loss of lifetime value of the customer
- Walking bad advert—word of mouth more believable than company-produced marketing messages
- Added costs of attracting new customers (estimated to be five times as much as looking after an existing one)
- Wasted resources in creating a company image
- Stressed staff dealing with dissatisfied customers may leave, giving recruitment and training costs

Designing Quality into Service

Awareness of how customers experience service is key to delivering the kind of service that delights, and like most things, planning outcome is fundamental to success. Services are more complex than products, as they are intangible processes, but also because there is an element that the customer must complete. This makes the relationship between the server and customer a critical element in service delivery, so service design needs to acknowledge this to understand the determinants of service quality and create an effective link between customer and service-provider staff. The communication time between customer and server has been identified as one of the most important dimensions of perceptions of quality and varies according to server, customer service, and environment. Hence, this element needs also to be planned in. Service waiting time builds customers' perceptions regarding the quality of a service event; long waiting times are perceived to indicate lack of responsiveness, so managing queuing by giving customers things to read, watch, or engage in is crucial.

Moments of Truth

Relationships generally begin as a transaction, with little long-term commitment on either side, but once the customer enters into repeat purchasing, there are likely to be things that delight and things that disappoint as the relationship builds. These occasions were called "Moments of Truth" by Jan Carlzon of Scandinavian Airlines.

Moments of truth—the points in the relationship with a customer where you have the opportunity to earn their true loyalty by engaging with them.

Moments of truth, although they may be positive, are more often negative in nature, but represent key turning points in the relationship. When a customer defects, losses are both hard and soft, as are the gains from loyalty and can be can be categorized into *Moments of Pain* and *Moments of Glory*.

Moments of truth, whether painful or glorious (Moments of pain and Moments of Glory), force a focus on the customer's experience (actual and desired), rather than the transactional relationship, which is usually taken for granted by the customer.

Marketers need to recognize those moments *and* understand how to make the brand stretch to meet customers' needs at every Moment of Truth.

Capitalizing on moments of truth and their nuances to the customer, marketing's role is to:

- Improve overall experience
- Provide richness of engagement and context
- Reduce friction

How to Identify Moments of Truth

Moments of truth can be anticipated by building customer personas that capture the goals, motivations, and barriers of your customers and prospects and by mapping the potential engagements customers have with the business.

Customer Personas

These are a powerful tool for thinking about the emotional needs of your customers and their behaviors, and this understanding will help you to identify Moments of Truth.

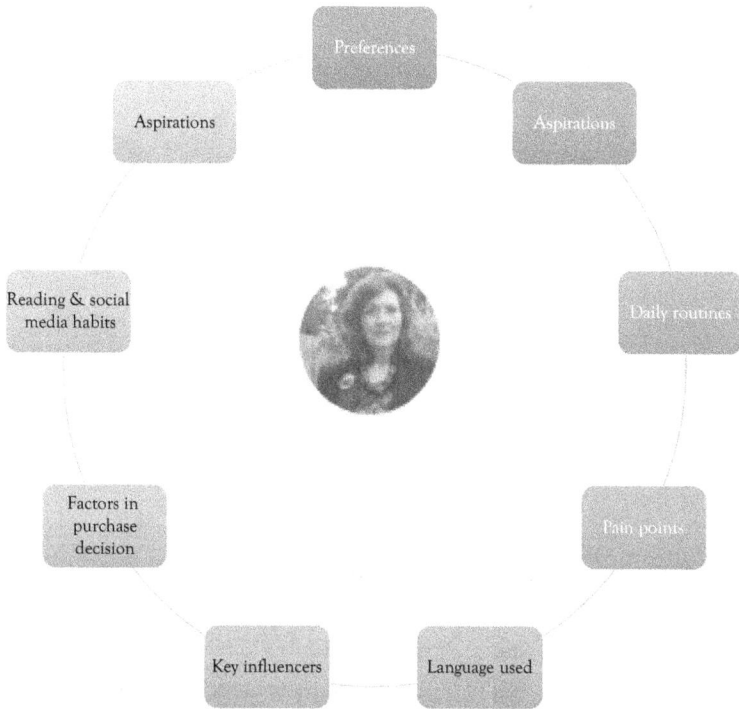

Figure 3.3 Customer persona example

Source: Adapted from https://getmintent.com/blog/customer-personas-impact-content-marketing/

Customer Journey Mapping

Consumers undergo a journey to becoming a customer, and with luck and good planning, a regular, recurring customer for the business.

This journey can be mapped: picturing how the journey is now and defining the future journey:

Mapping the customer journey requires evaluation of each customer touchpoint, some of which the business can control (e.g., messages and navigation tools on the website) and others the business cannot influence (such as review sites, blogs, and competitor promotions).

Most touchpoint evaluations assume a linear and direct relationship with the customer, and that customers encounter touchpoints meaningfully, and the consideration of touchpoints is so company-focused that touchpoints are categorized by functional area: marketing, operations, billing, and so on. The customer wants simple interaction, and a

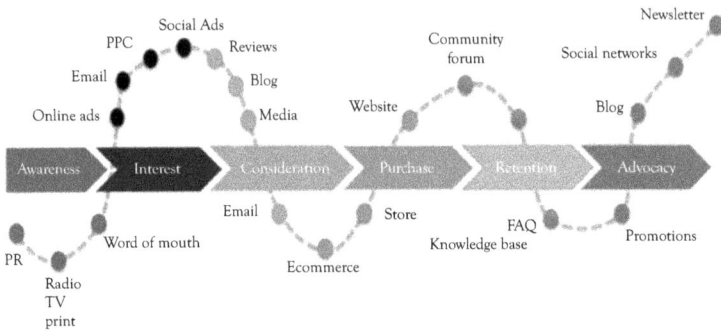

Figure 3.4 Sample customer journey

Source: https://econsultancy.com/blog/68958-the-five-key-steps-towards-understanding-the-customer-journey-and-where-most-marketers-are-stuck

holistic experience, not a multiplicity of contact from different areas of the business. A living customer experience journey map can help staff collaborate to inform, educate, and help the customer in ways that matter to them. Good understanding of the customer journey supports the ability to identify Moments of Truth, the customer drivers at these points, and the possible interactions.

Customer Insights

Persona development and customer journey mapping are driven by insight. These three approaches will help you to identify Moments of Truth:

Table 3.1 Approaches to identifying moments of truth

Research	Data	Internal experts
Existing research can identify points of greatest friction for customers. Net Promoter Score collected throughout the customer lifecycle is particularly valuable, as are in-depth interviews with customers.	Data underpins the customer journey mapping. From acquisition to advocacy, understanding the points at which the customer experience offers least (e.g., greatest points of churn) will help deliver quality.	Within the organization, customer-facing staff are a powerful resource that can be used to confirm what the research and data indicate.

How Customers Perceive Quality

Although the word quality is commonly used, we all have slightly different interpretations of what it means. It also encompasses something to do with value for money, and we all have different concepts of what offers value to us as individuals. No service provider sets out to deliver inferior service, but many fail to recognize the dimensions that matter to customers, so gaps emerge between the provider perspective and customer perspective.

How to Measure Quality

One model of service quality, known as the *gaps model*, identifies the components of service quality, provides a scale for measuring service quality (SERVQUAL), and suggests possible causes of service quality problems (Parasuraman, Zeithaml and Berry 1988).

The SERVQUAL model identifies five dimensions important to customers when evaluating service quality. Service providers who get these dimensions right are delivering service excellence and likely to earn customer loyalty and advocacy.

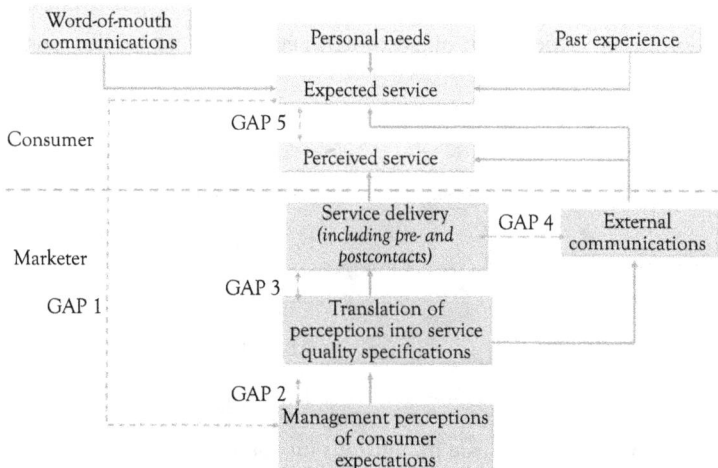

Figure 3.5 Model of service quality adapted from Zeithaml, Parasuraman, and Berry 1988

The five SERVQUAL dimensions also known as the RATER model are:

- *Reliability*: Ability to perform the promised service dependably and accurately
- *Assurance*: Knowledge and courtesy of employees and their ability to convey trust and confidence
- *Tangibles*: Appearance of physical facilities, equipment, personnel, and communication materials
- *Empathy*: Caring, individualized attention the firm provides its customers
- *Responsiveness*: Willingness to help customers and provide prompt service

Not All Dimensions Are Equal

All dimensions matter to customers, but with varying importance. Service providers need to discern customer priorities to effectively design their services while ensuring that all are demonstrated. SERVQUAL asks customers to assign 100 points across all five dimensions to establish priorities.

The following diagram shows that reliability and responsiveness are the dominant dimensions in customers' evaluation of service quality.

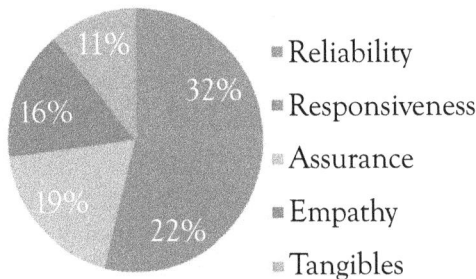

Figure 3.6 The five service dimensions customers care about reproduced with kind permission of Chris Arlen, President, revenue-IQ ~ selling smarter. richer results. Based on "Delivering Quality Service," by Valerie Zeithaml, A. Parasuraman and Leonard Berry.

Source: http://serviceperformance.com/the-5-service-dimensions-all-customers-care-about/

From an organizational perspective, there is clearly a decision to be made regarding the cost of ensuring all of the dimensions versus the gains in customer retention and turnover. In order to deliver a service that is both reliable and responsive, the organization needs to focus on both the process, which needs to be sufficiently robust to produce reliability, and on culture, which will provide responsiveness, and empathy. A servant leadership approach (see Chapter 4) within the organization it is likely to foster the kind of culture required to make staff keen to provide the best possible service for customers and to have authority to do so.

Employees, as well as managers, need to participate in designing customer service—they will have frontline contact with clients, so their input is vital, and their involvement in design will give them ownership, and they will want to make it work.

1. Listen to your customers by monitoring interactions. Ask questions such as: are these interactions related to the company's goals and objectives, or are they related to specific areas of concern such as customer attrition? This is where analytics comes into play for the contact center. Speech analytics identifies calls that are relevant for evaluation, and text analytics identifies e-mail and chat interactions that should be monitored.

2. Capture all of your customer feedback channels. Apply the same quality standard that is used for calls to text-based interactions such as e-mail and chat.

3. Ask your customer what they think. Instead of using your organization's internal metrics to measure the quality of a call, ask the customer: "What did you think of your experience and the agent you worked with?" or "Did your service experience match the promise made in our advertising?" It is very important to map high-quality interactions with your customers' expectations, comparing internal evaluation scores with customer scores.

4. Use quality monitoring to help agents improve skills. Evaluate interactions to identify skills gaps and provide individual learning opportunities where there are deficiencies.

5. Do not view agent development as a one-off activity. Provide continuous coaching that will help improve agent performance and productivity. Coaching is key to consistent customer service.

6. Measure your results and keep track of continuous feedback and evaluation to monitor and measure progress.

Expressing Quality

Worldwide, there are many awards for quality, and these assume greater importance in areas where is the perceived risk of purchase is greatest, such as medical, dentistry, or legal services, large item purchases such as cars, holidays, and houses. For such items, quality awards, such as the EFQM excellence awards, or ABTA/ATOL assurance in the travel Industry play a key role in decision making at the search and evaluation stages of the purchase decision, as they help overcome perceived risk. As more purchases take place online, customer perception of risk increases, as customers do not have a personal relationship upon which to build trust and confidence.

Quite apart from the global quality awards, companies seek to understand whether they are delivering satisfaction, delight, or disgust to customers by asking them to evaluate the service they have received. Online purchases are usually followed-up by an e-mail asking the customer to rate the service they have received and comment upon it. These links to websites that post reviews about people, businesses, products, or services. Services that do this include Feefo, Trustpilot, reviews.co.uk, TripAdvisor, Yell, and so on. One of the issues with such sites is that they contain user-generated content (postings are made by users, rather than professionals). This may mean that a negative review has been posted by a competitor, or a favorable one, by a family member, friend, or an employee, so objectivity maybe lacking.

Customers also suffer from review fatigue, as they are asked to evaluate every purchase they make, and some sites are quite demanding in terms of input, so experiences at either end of the spectrum appear, but perhaps average or expected service does not, providing a distorted picture.

One of the best and most trusted evaluation tools is NetPromoter or NPS, which measures customer experience and predicts business growth. This now provides the core measurement for customer experience management programs the world round. Part of its appeal is that it asks only one question: "How likely is it that you would recommend [brand] to a

Not at all likely					Neutral				Extremely likely	
0	1	2	3	4	5	6	7	8	9	10
		Detractor					Passive		Promoter	

% Promoters - % Detractors = NPS (Net Promoter Score)

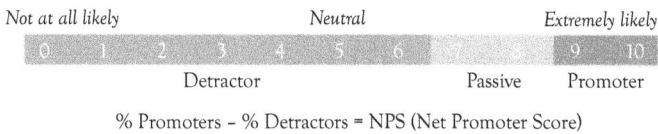

Figure 3.7 NetPromoter

friend or colleague?" This makes it simple for customers to respond, and response rates are high.

Respondents are grouped as follows:

- *Promoters* (score 9–10) are loyal enthusiasts who will keep buying and refer others, fueling growth.
- *Passives* (score 7–8) are satisfied, but unenthusiastic customers who are vulnerable to competitive offerings.
- *Detractors* (score 0–6) are unhappy customers who can damage your brand and impede growth through negative word-of-mouth.

Subtracting the percentage of detractors from the percentage of promoters yields the NPS, which can range from a low of –100 (if every customer is a detractor) to a high of 100 (if every customer is a promoter).

Quotations/Interviews from Key Practitioners/Leaders of Excellence Businesses

Quality means doing it right when no one is looking. Henry Ford, attributed, Hearts Touched with Fire.

People will sit up and take notice of you if you will sit up and take notice of what makes them sit up and take notice.
                                                    —Henry Selfridge

Your most unhappy customers are your greatest source of learning.
                                                    —Bill Gates, CEO Microsoft

Elon Musk, former CEO of PayPal, SpaceX founder, and current CEO of Tesla has this to say about feedback: "I think it's very important to have a feedback loop, where you're constantly thinking about what you've done and how you could be doing it better."

Tony Hsieh, founder and CEO of Zappos. "We take most of the money that we could have spent on paid advertising and instead put it back into the customer experience. Then we let the customers be our marketing."

Case studies analyzing good and weak aspects:

A rigid attitude might just be the antithesis of great customer service. Proving that they are a company that knows how to have a little fun, this next story from Sainsbury's supermarket highlights how your support team should spot great opportunities to do things that are quirky and out of the ordinary.

Lily Robinson (who insists that she is three-*and-a-half* years old) was quite confused by one of Sainsbury's products called tiger bread. In her eyes, the bread did not resemble a tiger at all, and in fact, looked very much like a giraffe.

It Is Hard to Disagree with Her!

With a little assistance from mum and dad, she wrote a letter to Sainsbury's customer service department.

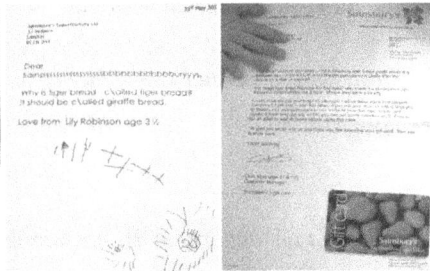

To her surprise, customer support manager Chris King (age 27 *and one-third*) told her that he could not agree more. He explained the origins of the name:

It's hard to disagree with her!
With a little assistance from mum and dad, she wrote a letter to Sainsbury's customer service department.

Figure 3.8 Example of Tiger bread and a customer interaction with Sainsbury's

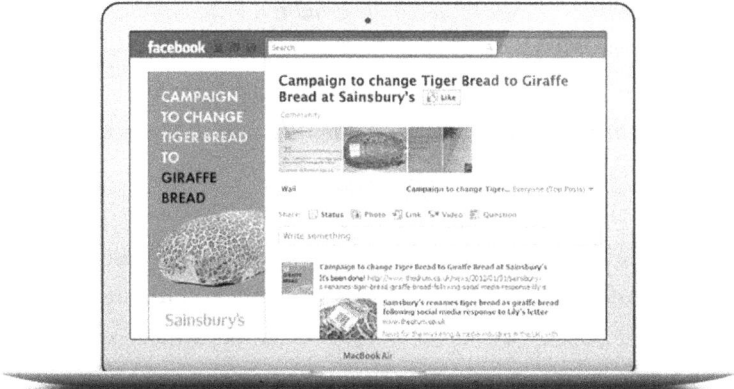

Figure 3.9 Facebook page on tiger bread

Figure 3.10 Sainsbury's answer

Figure 3.11 Trader Joe going above and beyond expectations

I think renaming tiger bread giraffe bread is a brilliant idea - it looks much more like the blotches on a giraffe than the stripes on a tiger, doesn't it? It is called tiger bread because the first baker who made it a loooong time ago thought it looked stripy like a tiger. Maybe they were a bit silly.

Lily's mum enjoyed the letters and posted them on her blog. Quickly, this cute correspondence became a viral hit, and the pressure was on for Sainsbury's to change the name of the product to the much more appropriate giraffe bread.

Knowing the customer was certainly right in this instance—and spotting an unusual opportunity to do something fun—Sainsbury's changed the name of the bread *and* put signs around their stores that give a humorous nod to Lily's original idea.

Trader Joe's Delivers (Literally)

An elderly man, 89 years of age, was snowed in at his Pennsylvanian home around the holidays, and his daughter was worried that he was not going to have access to enough food due to the impending storm and bad weather in the area. After calling multiple stores in a desperate attempt to find anyone who would deliver to her father's home, she finally found someone at Trader Joe's, who told her that they also do not deliver ... normally.

Given the extreme circumstance, they told her that they would gladly deliver directly to his home and even suggested additional delivery items that would fit perfectly with his special low-sodium diet.

After the daughter placed the order for the food, the employee on the phone told her that she did not need to worry about the price; the food would be delivered free of charge. The employee then wished her a Merry Christmas.

Less than 30 minutes later, the food was at the man's doorstep—free of charge!

In refusing to let red tape get in the way of a customer in need, Trader Joe's shows that customer service does not need to be about the fanfare, it can simply be about doing the right thing.

Horror Stories

Walmart's Pricing Blunder

Imagine that you walk into your local Walmart Lego set you want to buy for your son. You notice that the item at the store costs 35 percent more than the same exact Lego set on Walmart's own website.

That's exactly what happened to Clark Howard. But, when he asked the team to meet their company's online price, Walmart refused to price match, so he pulled out his phone and ordered the product online for an in-store pick-up.

Howard says, "My son and I stood there and watched as a different employee came a few minutes later, picked the item up off the shelf, and brought it back to the holding spot for pickup." Because Howard did not receive the e-mail confirmation from Walmart.com until the following day, he could not bring the item home that day, but had to go back to the store the next day—inconvenient, to say the least. Although Walmart does not require that store managers match online prices, it would have been the best (and only) response in this scenario.

Takeaway

When companies prioritize a policy above the needs of customers, it shows.

The golden rule—treat others the way you want to be treated—should trump any protocol. If you are not sure how to respond in a scenario, think about what is the kindest, most honest thing to do. This overarching ethos can easily prevent really bad customer service stories from happening on your watch.

Whirlpool's Negligence

For eight years, A New York Times column called *The Haggler* helped frustrated people manage bad customer experiences. Joanna Vintilla reached out to the column for help with a 216 U.S. dollars Whirlpool microwave that became a customer service problem.

The backstory: Vintilla had a Whirlpool-approved technician visit her house five times to fix her microwave. He had replaced four parts of the microwave within six months of Vintilla's purchase, and the technician said he already needed to replace some of those same parts again.

But, Vintilla could not get anyone at Whirlpool to help get a replacement for her defective microwave. In fact, Whirlpool's customer service team insisted she wait until the one-year warranty expired, and even then, they would have to send another technician and wait six months to consider the exchange.

Once *The Haggler* got involved, Whirlpool offered a refund with two stipulations: Vintilla would have to pay Whirlpool 75 U.S. dollars to dispose of the broken machine and sign a confidentiality clause. The whole debacle was written up in one of the most respected newspapers in the country, which did not do Whirlpool's reputation any favors.

Takeaway

Confidentiality clauses—especially for purchases like a 216 U.S. dollars microwave—are the quickest way to end a relationship with a customer. Likewise, asking customers to pay for a company's mistakes is nothing short of insulting. Both tactics magnify an already upsetting issue.

End of Chapter Summary

This chapter has explored the importance of quality, both of product and service, to establishing the customer relationship. It considers the costs both of achieving quality and of having to put it right when it has gone wrong.

It provides suggestions for gaining a deeper understanding of the customer perception of quality and some consideration of evaluation tools that are available to support this understanding.

End of Chapter Review Questions

	Show as a spectrum					
Quality	High			Low		
How important is quality to you?						
How important is quality of service to you?						
How important is quality to your organization?						

How important is quality of service to your customers?						
How well do you understand the importance of quality?						
How much do your customers value a specific standard of quality?						
To what extent are your customers concerned about quality?						
What level of complaints do you receive from customers about quality issues?						
How you know whether your customers are satisfied with the quality of product or service?						
Does getting zero complaints interest you?	Yes			No		

References

http://emeraldinsight.com/doi/abs/10.1108/02656719410074297?journal
Code=ijqrm

http://dive-group.com/about-us/why-service-excellence-is-important/

http://business.uzh.ch/professorships/som/stu/Teaching/Teaching/
HeskettJonesLovemanSasserSchlesinger1994.pdf

http://conduithub.com/blog/what-are-moments-of-truth-and-how-do-you-
identify-them

http://serviceperformance.com/the-5-service-dimensions-all-customers-care-about/

https://researchgate.net/profile/Valarie_Zeithaml/publication/225083802_
SERVQUAL_A_multiple_Item_Scale_for_measuring_consumer_
perceptions_of_service_quality/links/5429a4540cf2

7e39fa8e6531/SERVQUAL-A-multiple-Item-Scale-for-measuring-consumer-
perceptions-of-service-quality.pdf

https://salesforce.com/hub/service/famous-customer-service-quotes/

https://helpscout.net/10-customer-service-stories/#one

https://helpscout.net/blog/bad-customer-service-stories/

Gronrros, C. 2016. *Service Management and Marketing: Managing the Service
Profit Logic.*

Lehtinen, J.R. 1983. "Customer Oriented Service System." *Service Management
Institute*, 1734–49. Working Paper, Helsinki, Finland.

Parasuraman, A., A.V. Zeithaml, and L.L. Berry. 1985. "A Conceptual Model
of Service Quality and Its Implications for Future Re-Search." *The Journal of
Marketing*, pp. 41–50, 49.

Soteriou, A.C., and R.B. Chaser. 1998. "Linking the Customer Contact Model
to Service Quality." *Journal of Operations Management* 16, pp. 495–508, 497.

CHAPTER 4

Establish Trust

Chapter Objectives

- To appreciate the role trust plays as part of the brand
- To understand how trust is created and how easily trust can be broken
- To understand the role of pricing in trust
- To appreciate the way service recovery can support trust
- To identify means of recovering trust
- To understand how trust in staff can deliver the responsiveness required
- To identify trust-exposed industries

Chapter Profile

This chapter explores the importance for consumers to be able to trust the brands that they buy. It examines the role of trust in the decision-making process and in building loyalty. Trust is built up slowly over a period of time, in much the same way as brand equity is established, and is also a key element in brand equity.

Trust in a brand goes deeper than a transactional understanding that the organization will make good on its promises; it encompasses the entire behavior of the brand, extending into whether the brand upholds the values expressed throughout its communications. So, trust can be broken by activities that do not have a direct effect on the customers' experience of using or purchasing the product or service, such as the way in which the brand treats its supply chain members or the way in which they treat their staff or contribute to the economies of the places they do business by paying taxes or engaging with the local community.

If customers are to embrace your brand as a *lovemark* by forming a deep, engaged relationship with it, trust must be a foundation stone. Brands need to have an understanding of how all of their actions may be perceived by their various customer segments and ensure authenticity of their actions with their company mission and messages they put out at all customer touchpoints. Information at the right stage in the purchase process plays an important role in building trust.

Trust is created or destroyed at every touchpoint, so organizations need to evaluate the entire marketing mix to understand how to build trust and identify potential trip wires in order to deliver confidence.

As any organization grows, it wrestles to balance empowerment with centralization of control, and building a culture of trust among the workforce is a vital element of managing this balance. This tension between empowered frontline staff and kind of control that can promote quality often manifests itself as what might be described as *unnamed elephants*, which, if they remain unnamed, undermine the trust in the organization, and develop factions that can create friction internally, which customers will sense from inconsistencies in the organization as it performs its services. So, trust in the brand needs to be built from the inside out.

Key Terms

Perceived risk: the risk—either financial or in relation to their self-concept that customers feel in making a purchase. For B2C, this may include the possible negative comments from friends and family. In B2B, professional buyers may fear losing their jobs for making what are seen to be risky or unwise decisions, hence the saying "you never get fired for buying IBM," a brand that is perceived as being top quality, and therefore safe.

Touchpoints

A point of contact or interaction, especially between a business and its customers or consumers.

"Every touchpoint must reflect, reinforce, and reiterate your core brand strategy."

Any point at which the customer connects with the organization, including staff, website, vans, and so on. These need to present a uniform message to the customer, and all need to convey the brand meaning consistently.

Level of Involvement

Level of involvement is the degree of information processing and the amount of importance a consumer attaches to a product while purchasing it. In other words, it shows how involved the customer is toward a product personally, socially and economically.

There are two types of involvement, high and low:

Low involvement: Usually, these products involve a low level of risk or no risk and are inexpensive most of the times. Most of the time, consumers buy these products automatically. Examples of low involvement products are matchbox, toothpaste, snacks, and so on. For example, when a consumer buys a matchbox, he just picks up any matchbox that he sees in the store. Here, the purchase is automatic. When a consumer buys toothpaste, every brand has the same utility except for the preference of the consumer. Here, there is no risk involved even if he or she buys a toothpaste that is not the preferred brand.

High involvement: Usually, these products involve a high level of risk and are most probably expensive. Examples of high involvement products are car, diamonds, house, and so on. For example, when a consumer is buying a car, he or she will research the various models, different specifications, and other factors of all the cars that fall in his or her budget before making a decision. This is because there is a high risk involved, as he or she is spending a lot of money on the good.

Definition

Organizational Trust

The global evaluation of an organisation's trustworthiness, as perceived by the employee. Organizational trust is defined as an employee's feeling of confidence that the organization will perform actions that are beneficial, or at least not, detrimental, to him or her. (Tan & Tan 2000)

Table 4.1 Trust drivers adapted from Edelman

Operational trust attributes	Societal trust attributes
• Offers high-quality products or services. • Has transparent open business practices. • Communicates frequently and honestly on the state of its business. • Delivers consistent financial returns to investors. • Has highly regarded and widely admired top leadership. • Is an innovator of new products, services or ideas? • Ranks on a global list of top companies. • Partners with NGOs, government, and third parties to address societal issues.	• Listens to customer needs and feedback. • Takes responsible actions to address an issue or crisis. • Places customers ahead of profits. • Treats employees well. • Has ethical business practices. • Works to protect and improve the environment. • Addresses society's needs in its everyday business. • Creates programs that positively impact the local community.

What Makes Up Trust?

The Edelman Trust Index is an average of countries' trust in the institutions of government, business, media, and NGOs taken across 27 countries worldwide. This shows a rise in the levels of distrust worldwide, with media inspiring the lowest levels of trust around the world, and NGOs the highest.

Edelman's trust research indicates that a trustworthy company must combine operating efficiency with social responsibility, dividing the 16 trust drivers into *societal* and *operational* clusters.

Information as a Determinant of Trust

Customers need information to help them make their purchase decisions. An organization that is open and truly thinks about what information customers will need at each stage of the decision-making process and where they are likely to want to access such information is likely to inspire trust. Conversely, an organization that conceals information or makes it hard to find may create suspicion among its target audience.

The following figure indicates the different types of information required at each stage of the purchase process and how this varies for different product categories.

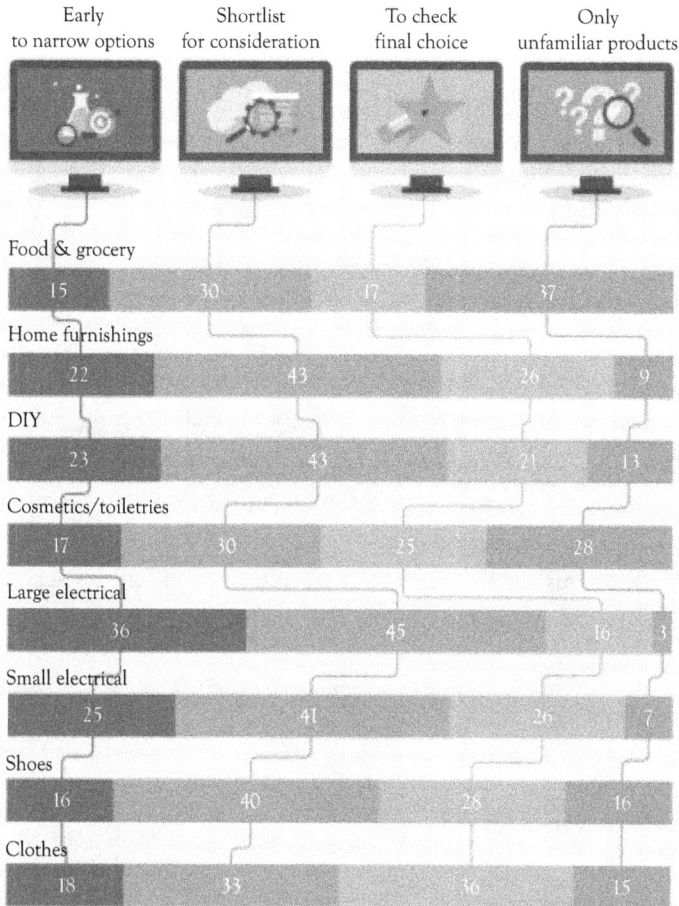

Figure 4.1 The point in the purchase when process information is most needed by product category reproduced with kind permission from (https://issuu.com/shoppercentric/docs/wo30_sst2018?e=23309330/58125242)

Creating Internal Trust

Internal branding enables and motivates employees to not only keep the brand promise, but to *live* it. This requires employees to be involved in the process of brand development, to be knowledgeable about the brand; businesses must inspire them to feel enthusiastic about the brand to create behavior that supports the brand. Brands grow from the inside out, and for authenticity, internal and external brand must relate to one another and tell a consistent story to generate trust and increased sales. A brand that is clearly understood by all employees can achieve a sharp image in the minds of its customers. Employees must be involved in the branding process at the outset, with representatives from different business units, rather than ad hoc, as is often the case. Early integration of employees with the brand strategy gives understanding and acceptance of the brand strategy, and they contribute valuable input to the success of the brand strategy when they recognize its meaning and benefits.

Internal branding expresses the brand strategy for the target group employee, demonstrating the brand identity in staff selection and development. The goal of internal branding is to guide employees toward brand-supporting behavior so that the customer feels employees are communicating the brand promise.

Lack of trust in the internal brand can originate in the actions of a supervisor who has not bought into the brand and undermines the

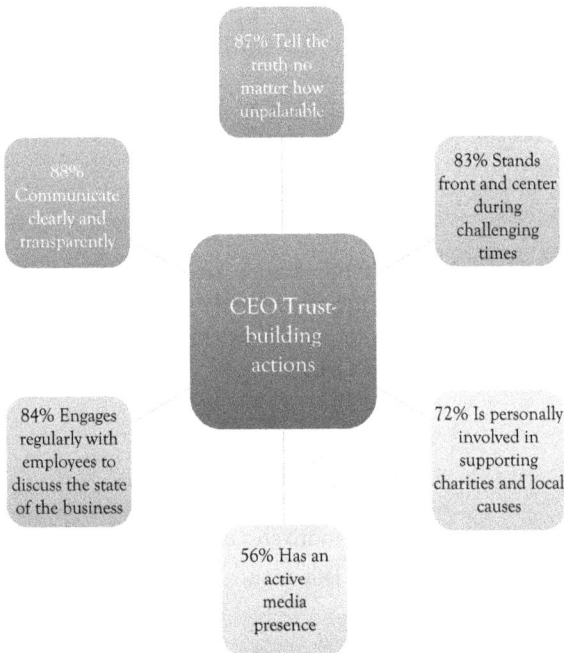

87% Tell the truth no matter how unpalatable

88% Communicate clearly and transparently

83% Stands front and center during challenging times

CEO Trust-building actions

84% Engages regularly with employees to discuss the state of the business

72% Is personally involved in supporting charities and local causes

56% Has an active media presence

Figure 4.2 Actions a CEO can take to build trust in themselves and their company

management, or it may be inherent in a culture that discourages discussion and hides conflict. Any act of bad management erodes trust, so it is vital that management stays true to its word at all times, or the lack of trust among staff will become apparent to customers.

Inconsistent Standards

Consistent standards applied throughout the organization give rise to a feeling of fairness, building trust, so favoritism, or allowing one individual to bend the rules, will make people jump to the worst conclusion. There may be a temptation to let talented employees behave differently to retain them, but this undermines team spirit and neglects the cynicism you engender in the rest of the organization.

Managers understand that dishonesty demands immediate censure, but often, most disruptive behavior is not so obvious, and therefore hard to manage.

Customers care about the way a company treats its staff and choose to do business with those with a good reputation for staff care. Parcelforce (which delivers for Marks and Spencer, John Lewis, and Hamleys) staff who are unable to work due to illness can be charged up to £250 if they are unable to find cover because they are classified as owner drivers. For such reputable retailers, this is an example of an organization failing to think things through and risking alienation of customers by losing congruence with their values. Customer also expect this to permeate throughout the supply chain, especially since the UK horse meat scandal of 2013, so Parcelforce needs to do a rethink if its bad practices are not to taint their clients' brands.

Trust in the Brand

Trust is one of the elements that makes up reputation, and if the brand is to act as to attract customers to do business with the organization, reputation is vital. Trust deepens as service delivery meets expectations, or disintegrates as a result of broken promises, so organizations need to understand its role in service delivery, and in marketing.

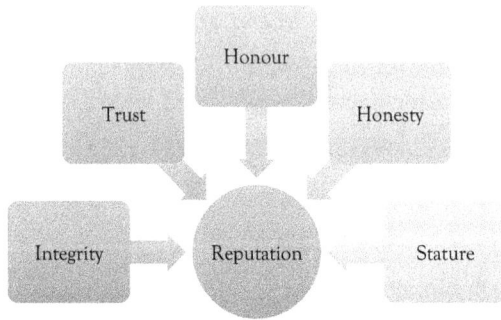

Figure 4.3 The components of trust

The strategy of navigating trust in today's complex market is not easy. The habitat that brands and businesses exist in is visibly and rapidly transforming. When the environment is unstructured and ambiguous, brands often struggle to come to grips with a unifying strategy.

Trust is the force that binds brands to their ecosystem, helping shape its identity and building relationships. Without building, maintaining, or refurbishing trust constantly, brands will invariably weaken, wither, or even fade.

TRA Research presents its second interactive event—Trust Conference 2017. The conference is a platform to generate conversations on the essence of trust and to further delve on the significance of building brands to last.

(http://trustadvisory.info/tra/trustconference2017.php)

Figure 4.4 Summary of 2017 Trust Conference

Trust in the brand has become an issue of such importance that there is now an annual conference on trust, that, in 2017, stated the following:

This recognizes the complexity of trust, the need for it to be part of the brand identity, and the foundation for relationships the brand forms. The rise in ethical consumerism has created a need for brands to demonstrate their trustworthiness by engaging in corporate social responsibility (CSR) activities, in part, to support the legal obligation for them to have a CSR policy, but also in large part to engage the hearts and minds of consumers. Millennials especially aspire to be ethical consumers, and to work for ethical businesses, and given that they are the consumers of the future, organizations need to be listening to them.

Most brands now dedicate an area of their website to things they do on a global, national, or local basis to improve the environments they work and operate in and to support causes linked to their corporate activities. These range in scale from British Petroleum, BP, a global player in energy and oil exploration, who have several pages of their website dedicated to sustainability in its various guises, down to small independent retailers, such as The Alnwick Studio hairdressers, whose staff regularly has a team-building exercise on the local Northumberland beach, clearing flotsam and jetsam to improve the local environment for locals and tourists.

Interestingly shown in Table 4.7, of these top 10 trusted brands, none has a particularly long history—perhaps indicating trends in what people buy or perhaps acknowledging a preference for innovation in purchasing habits. Mintel, the research agency, has produced reports on trust in the food industries.

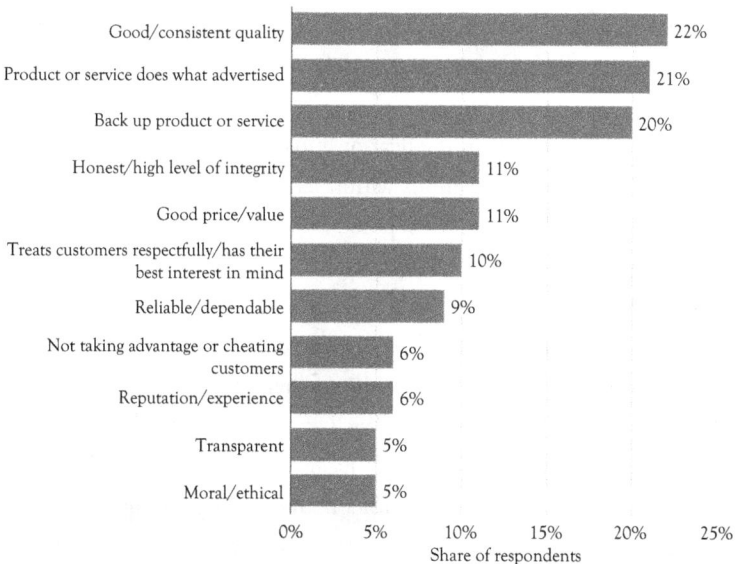

Figure 4.5 Definitions of trust from Canadian consumers reproduced by kind permission of (https://statista.com/statistics/446408/definitions-of-brand-trust-according-to-consumers-canada/)

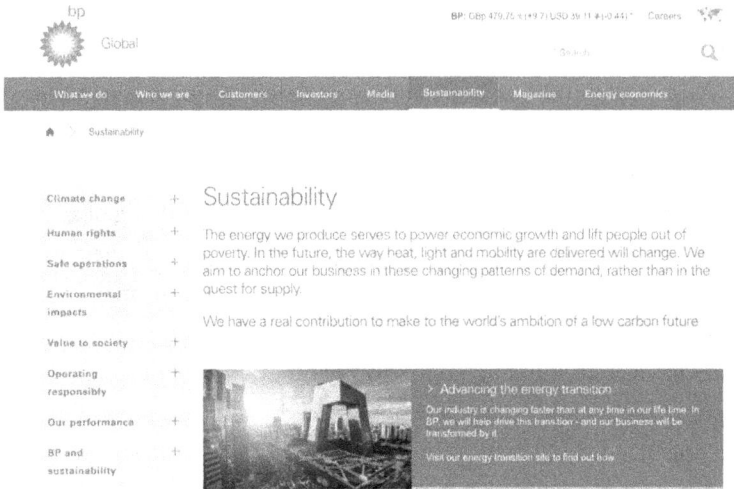

Figure 4.6 BP Sustainability page (accessed on February 12, 2018). Reproduced with kind permission of BP

Just 53 percent of UK consumers trust the food and drink industry to ensure food and drink is safe for consumption, plummeting to 39 percent amongst beauty and personal care consumers. Mintel blog http://mintel.com/blog/consumer-market-news/the-truth-about-trust-strengthening-consumer-trust (accessed February 14, 2018)

Trust applies not only to the relationships that organizations form with consumers, but also organizations within its supply chain. The horse meat scandal in the United Kingdom exposed huge flaws in many supply chains and has prompted a much-needed overhaul of all supply chains, especially in the food industry. It is no longer justifiable to say that what happens in supplier organizations is not the responsibility of the end provider; all companies need to ensure the integrity of their supply chain by checking that they have the same value set, as well as ensuring that there is an effective audit trail for any product. Tesco has now committed to offering longer-term contracts with suppliers, rather than pursuing the cheapest cost for each purchase. This highlights the advantages for retailers and manufacturers to communicate responsible approaches to business to the market through advertising, social media, and other forms. Those that clearly outline their values, and live up to them are more likely to achieve a sustainable business.

Logo	Name	Value ($ M)
1 Go gle	Google	300,063
2	Apple	300,595
3 amazon	Amazon	207,594
4 Microsoft	Microsoft	200,987
5 Tencent 腾讯	Tencent	178,990
6 facebook	Facebook	162,106
7 VISA	Visa	145,611
8	Mcdonald's	126,044
9 Alibaba Group	Alibaba Group	113,401
10	AT&T	106,698

Figure 4.7 Top trusted brands worldwide adapted from (https://rankingthebrands.com/The-Brand-Rankings.aspx?rankingID=6)

Only 24 percent of consumers see the supermarkets as caring for British farmers while nearly half (45 percent) disagree. The finding is especially concerning considering that almost seven in ten (68 percent) consumers view it as the duty of the retailers to support British farmers/growers. Mintel, Consumer Trust in Food (2013)

Consumers no longer automatically trust organizations. Mintel research shows just 25 percent of the people using a device to access national newspapers online say that the content on these websites is trustworthy. The balance of power has shifted as a result of social media, and

Increase in trust ⟶

Paying expected levels of tax	42%
Responsible behaviour	42%
Increased transparency about operations and business practices	34%
Putting customers at heart of business	32%
Consistent level of service and quality	30%
Driving growth in the economy	24%
Addressing society's needs	18%

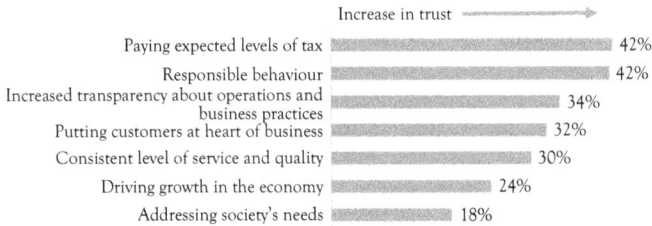

Figure 4.8 Factors likely to drive trust in businesses in Britain 2015 reproduced with kind permission of The Institute of Customer Service, UK

GoCompare

Keep your Car Insurance premiums on ice

Are you being taken for a ride by car insurance renewal prices?
Avoid expensive auto renewals and shop around today!

Figure 4.9 Screenshot from a speculative e-mail sent on July 31, 2018, showing the cynical attitude of insurance companies

consumers now instantly question and take brands to task when their actions cause concern or confusion. However, many consumers—especially the younger group—expect companies to take a more proactive, high-tech approach when it comes to demonstrating increasing transparency. One in five 20- to 24-year-old British shoppers would like online retailers to show videos showing how the products they sell are made.

Actions of some industries undermine any trust people might feel; the insurance industry receives regular criticism from consumers because they offer good deals for customers to switch their insurance, only to hike the price at renewal time, presumably in the hope that consumers will just continue to pay. When challenged, the response is often a reduction in

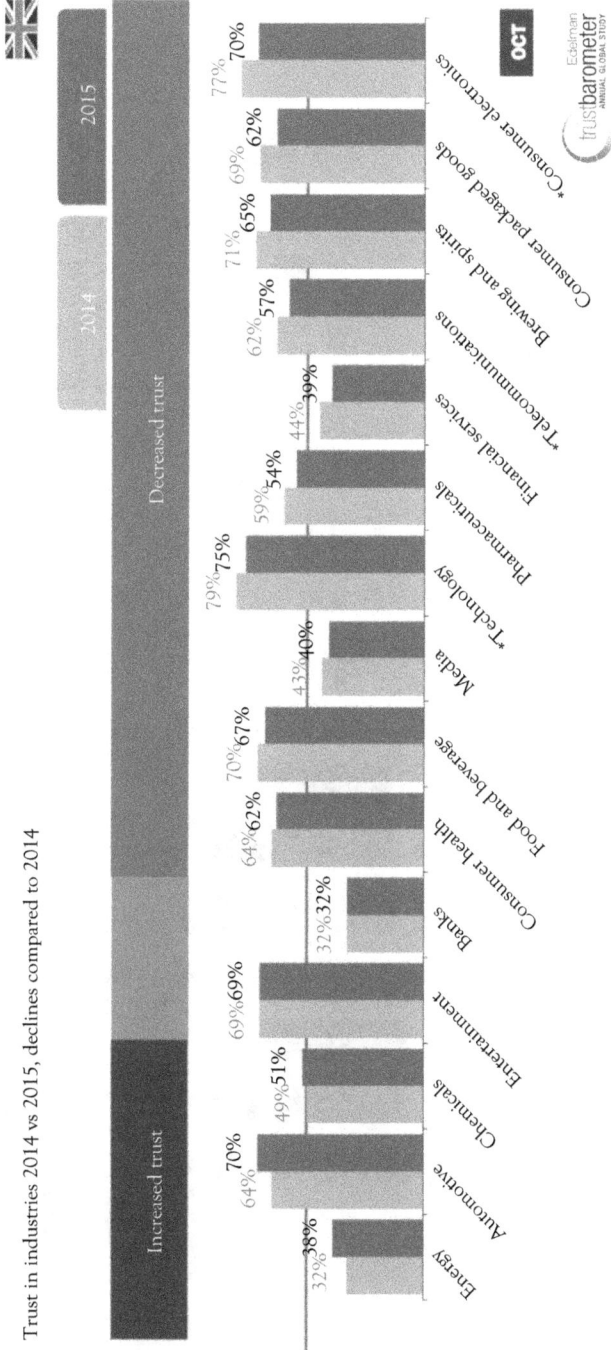

Trust in industries 2014 vs 2015, declines compared to 2014

Increased trust   Decreased trust

2014   2015

Industry	2014	2015
*Consumer electronics	77%	70%
Consumer packaged goods	69%	62%
Brewing and spirits	71%	65%
*Telecommunications	62%	57%
Financial services	44%	39%
Pharmaceuticals	59%	54%
*Technology	79%	75%
Media	43%	40%
Food and beverage	70%	67%
Consumer health	64%	62%
Banks	32%	32%
Entertainment	69%	69%
Chemicals	49%	51%
Automotive	64%	70%
Energy	32%	38%

Figure 4.10 Trust in industries Reproduced with kind permission of Edelman Trust Barometer

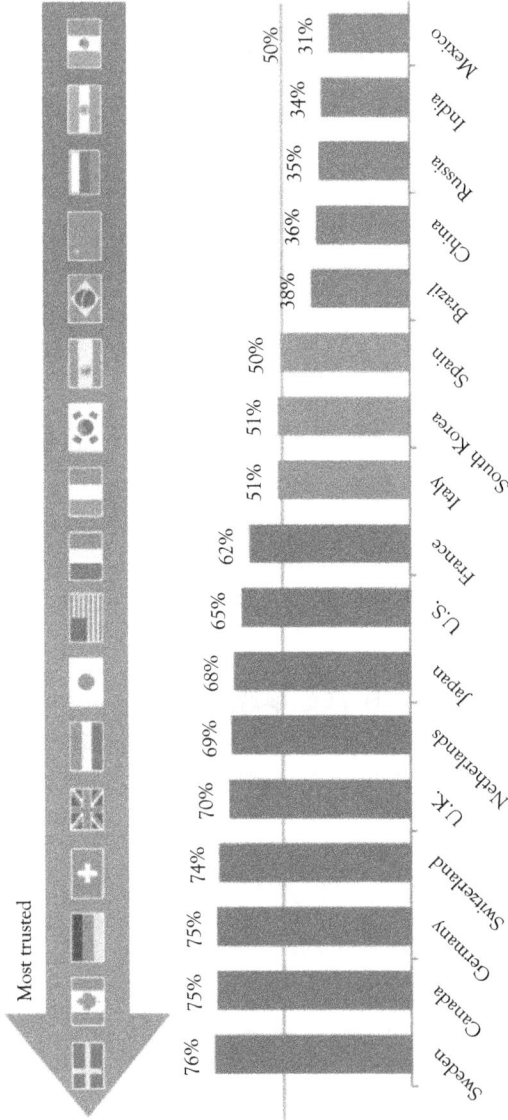

Figure 4.11 *Country of origin: trust in companies headquartered in the aforementioned countries; BRIC countries remain distrusted Reproduced with kind permission of Edelman Trust Barometer*

the price in order to meet a lower quote that the customer has obtained from competitors—almost an admission that they were intending to over-charge, until rumbled. These companies appear not to value a longer-term relationship and are not only missing out on the benefits that might derive from that, but also earning themselves a bad reputation in the shorter term.

The home country of a business also plays a role in trust for busi-nesses, as shown by the following table; this may be an explanation for some businesses choosing to locate in countries that are viewed more favorably, even though this could be seen as inauthentic.

Dealing with Feedback as a Means of Building Trust

Patrick Lencioni in his five dysfunctions of a team uses a pyramid to show the levels at which teams disintegrate:

If the pyramid is inverted to show a functional team, trust becomes the foundation, so establishing internal trust with the team is a key tenet of service excellence. Customers sense that strong foundation and feel safe to place their trust in the organization and its staff.

This echoes Robert Greenleaf's concept of servant leadership, which uses trust in front line to justify empowerment of action for them.

Trust enables the organization to establish authenticity through:

- Inviting and responding positively to feedback;
- Growing and learning more by being open to receive information;
- Teaching and serving others;
- Empathize because the focus is outward rather than inward;
- Being human.

Figure 4.12 Lencionis's five dysfunctions of a team

Trust enables deepening relationships by removing politics and silos, creating an organization within which people feel safe and which is welcoming to customers. Trust catalyzes excellence for your organization, giving greater freedom, flexibility, room for individual growth, and a platform for excellence.

For customers, in the past, giving feedback usually required a significant amount of courage, as it was rarely openly invited and often seen as negative. In recent years, it has become common practice for organizations to invite customer comment through surveys online or offline that offer the chance of entry to a prize draw or some similar incentive. There has also been a surge in the use of Feefo, Trustpilot, TripAdvisor, and so on where customers have the opportunity to evaluate and comment upon the service they receive from various organizations.

The way in which an organization deals with feedback says a great deal about its confidence to deliver excellence and also about its openness and willingness to improve. Positive comments give a great opportunity to reward the customer, either by giving some sort of incentive, such as a voucher or discount offer, or simply by thanking them and celebrating what they have shared.

Negative comments, which can feel hurtful, need to be viewed by the organization in a constructive manner. In essence, a customer who feels they can make a negative comment is really saying that they like most of what the organization has done, but have been disappointed by one experience or one aspect of the service. Such comments can be the starting point for improving the service overall or finding ways to innovate and keep the service offering fresh. In either case, it is vital, that is the organizational response is expressed in positive terms, thanking the customer for their useful observation, suggesting that the organization has taken it on board, and indicating any actions inspired by the comment.

People will forget what you said. People will forget what you did. But people will never forget how you made them feel.

—Maya Angelou

Trust and Purchase Involvement

Many factors influence a consumer's behavior. Well-informed and experienced consumers often make quick purchase decisions, while other consumers need to research and consider the decision before making a purchase. The *level of involvement* reflects:

- the importance of the purchase, in terms of cost
- the amount of information required to make a decision
- personal taste in the consumption of the product
- reflected status of the consumer when using the product

The level of involvement in purchase decisions runs along a spectrum from routine purchases (with limited involvement) to complex decisions demanding extensive research and close involvement. Involvement varies by purchaser, although many products, such as cars and houses, are typically higher in involvement because of high costs or high risk of status. For customers, the *perceived risk* of purchasing is high; therefore, the decision-making process is more complex and thorough. Novice consumers in a sector are typically more involved than repeat purchasers.

Whichever end of the involvement spectrum consumers are at for a purchase, trust plays a key role. At the lower end of the spectrum, for routine, or previously purchased items, consumers' trust is based on a satisfactory previous experience with the brand and its associated service. For more premium items, trust is built through perceptions of the brand,

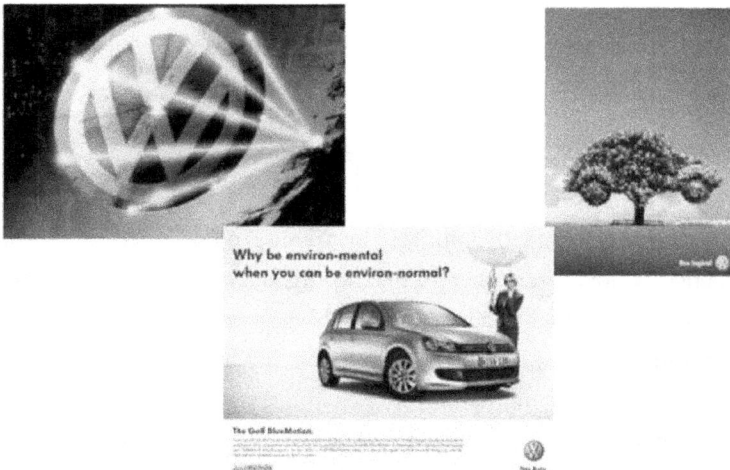

Figure 4.13 Sample of Volkswagen's environment-friendly advertisements prior to the 2015 scandal

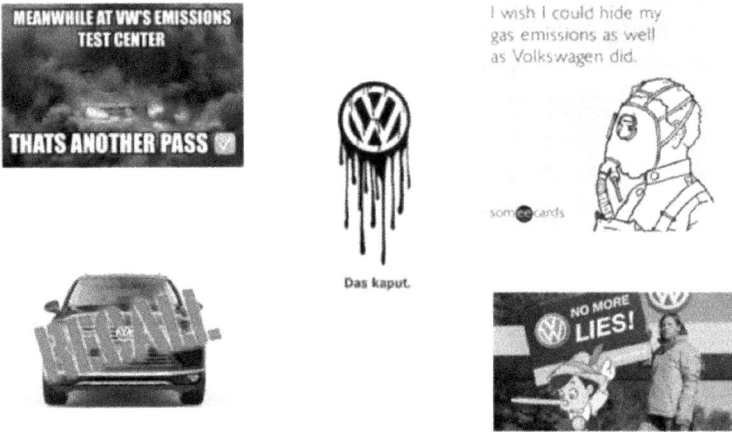

Figure 4.14 *Selection of spoof advertisements appearing shortly after the Volkswagen emissions scandal*

gained across all *touchpoints* of the organization, as well as formed by contact with friends and family who have experienced the brand.

Volkswagen cars are a high involvement product that seriously damaged sales, losing a third of its share price when it was found to have misrepresented vehicle emissions to the public and eventually admitted that 11 million vehicles around the world were fitted with a device that allowed them to cheat emissions testing, with emissions rates up to 40 times higher in daily use than in tests. Cars were recalled, at a cost to Volkswagen of €6.5 billion (£4.8 billion). The damage to the trust in the brand was all the greater because Volkswagen had marketed heavily the trust in the brand, which was then broken.

Trust and Pricing

Customers are frequently infuriated by promises of low price deals on airline tickets. An air-travel survey by TripAdvisor.com found 71 percent of travelers are annoyed by add-on fees for baggage and seat selection, which used to be included in the fare. Another study by the Chief Marketing Officer Council found that almost two in five travelers were stressed out by the process of researching and finding deals. Customers want transparency: they want to see the full cost of a trip clearly before checkout, and not encounter add-ons for baggage, seat booking, and other aspects.

Making a like-for-like comparison is a challenge, and short of tot-ting up with a calculator and notepad, there is no practical way of doing it. Often, low-cost carriers dominate the online search; yet, at the final checkout, costs are often the same or higher. This lack of transparency in pricing contributes to mistrust in the industry. Booking fees, baggage charges, and a host of optional service fares are now common industry practice. Baggage fees were last year worth more than 3.3 billion U.S. dollars to the American aviation industry, while fees for reservation charges contributed U.S. airlines 2.38 billion U.S. dollars in 2011, according to the Bureau of Transportation Statistics. As a result, ticket prices that initially appear good value rise rapidly on inclusion of hidden extras at the checkout. "Additional fees for things like baggage allowance and seat selection can be above and beyond what it costs the airline (to offer these services)," says Chris Gray, deputy editor of U.K.-based consumer maga-zine Which? Travel. "These are often sprung on customers at the end of a long booking process." The airline industry was one of the last to unbun-dle its services; the consumer can now choose what they pay for, rather than having a bundle of services such as in-flight meals or entertainment that they do not use.

Baggage Fees

Most budget airlines make a charge for noncarry-on luggage. With the vast majority of established airline industry players, one item of baggage (up to a certain weight) and one carry on is permitted before a fee is incurred. Ironically, on many low-cost carriers, so many passengers opt to take only cabin baggage that cabin crew are offering to stow cabin bags in the hold to make space.

Two U.S. airlines, Spirit and *Allegiant*, have recently begun to charge passengers for carry-on cases. Such policies are immensely frustrating for consumers who have more than one bag or an item of luggage deemed too big for the plane cabin. People are also suspicious of the airlines' weighing systems. The airlines' defense is that these fees give more choice and potentially save customers' money. Without the option to pay for baggage requirements separately, this extra cost would automatically be added to the price of the ticket.

Seat Selection Charges

One of the more recent additional cost options to come to the fore is a premium to reserve flight seats. In the United States, Delta, American Airlines, and low-cost carriers U.S. Airways, Frontier, Spirit, and Allegiant have implemented charges for *preferred seating*. In Europe, budget carrier *Ryanair* began offering specific seats at an extra cost and has now been joined by their rival EasyJet.

This was formerly free, so the change is irritating, especially for families who have to pay to select seats together. It can hardly be desirable for staff or other passengers to have children sitting away from their parents. Airlines compare this seat booking to sports and theater venues where obstructed view seats are cheaper than prime seats.

Credit and Debit Card Surcharges

A common complaint of those booking plane tickets online is the unavoidable charges that often accompany paying for flights by a debit or credit card. The U.K. government's trading and competition authority, the Office of Fair Trading, recently ruled that debit card surcharges must be included in the headline price of flights. Budget carriers, including Ryanair and Whizz Air, have amended their online booking policies to reflect this. But elsewhere, the practice remains. While retailers incur some costs for processing card payments, the charges passed on to the consumer are often excessive.

The Enemies of Trust

Trust is an elusive concept, hard to earn, yet easily undermined by seemingly small issues. While the following points may seem obvious, we have all experienced brands that fail on at least one of these fronts and have no doubt voted with our feet.

> *Misrepresentation*, or lying is the fastest way to lose the trust of even loyal customers. Making promises that are not kept, either as part of the initial brand promise or as part of a subsequent transaction, will destroy credibility very quickly, damaging relationships, and the potential for successful business.

Failing to respond to customer queries at any of the organizational touch-points conveys the message that the customer is unimportant to you. It is not a coincidence that the RATER model explored in Chapter 3 contains responsiveness as a key measure of customer satisfaction.

Late response is almost as bad as no response and can cause as much damage, so designing a process that will prompt timely response is important.

Poor-quality products, just as much as poor-quality service is frustrating for customers, and again, promises made by the brand in terms of product quality need to be matched by performance that meets customer expectations.

Unclear identity creates a confusing relationship for customers, so establishing a solid brand for the organization, with a consistent set of communications materials at all customer touchpoints ensures that you present a consistent message, and customers are confident about the organization they are dealing with.

Inconsistent messages between groups of stakeholders, often caused by weak managers telling people what they think they want to hear, rather than giving the facts. Message consistency comes from thinking through priorities, working out how best to present them coherently, realistically and honestly, and cascading this through the managerial team.

How Trust in the Brand Is Built

Table 4.2 Twelve tips for creating trust adapted from https://forbes. com/sites/forbesagencycouncil/2016/09/19/12-ways-new-companies-can-build-brand-trust/2/#434efa95416d

1. Speak to customers in an authentic, human voice	While the brand should sound authoritative, it should also be approachable and human. Conversational content helps messages act as an extension of the people that make the brand. Real-life interactions and authentic dialogue build trust. Mintel Inspire's Trend Human discusses how artisan, man-made goods with individual characteristics are often prized over mass-manufactured alternatives. This negativity about mass production can give smaller manufacturers an edge in the short term. Many mass-produced products now highlight the human element

(Continued)

Table 4.2 (Continued)

	—maybe a farmer, company owner, or production line workers in their communications in an attempt to humanize mass manufacturing. McDonald's have used images of a traditional farmer on a tractor to suggest their food is home grown (Mintel Trust in Food 2013).
2. Establish a friendship	Building brand trust as a new company is akin to a new friendship, with no knowledge on either side: there is heavy investment early on, respectfully learning their feelings and what is important to them. Mindfulness of the impact of each interaction with new customers builds brand trust.
3. Treat your first client like a VIP	Exceed customer satisfaction, show them that your company will do whatever it takes to gain their trust and keep them happy. That initial foundation of strong connections with customers forms a platform for referrals and advocates.
4. Solicit and value feedback	Asking for and valuing feedback (a quick survey, a social media follow, or an online review) engages customers and makes them feel valued. Online reviews play an increasingly important role in the buying decision, especially for online purchases. Companies need to encourage and monitor the feedback they are receiving and respond with transparency.
5. Capture founder authenticity	Telling the product and company story demonstrates the passion invested in the product. Sharing the thoughtful design process, prototypes, and failures can build emotional connections and earn the buy-in of new customers. Few large corporations can tap into this kind of story.
6. Offer great customer service	In any relationship, trust is created by showing care, dependability, and honesty; the same is true when creating brand trust. Providing customers with the best customer service consistently and giving a perk every once in a while meets the brand promise and builds trust.
7. Create an experience	Branding has shifted from marketers to people, so brands need to provide the context for them to do so. Authentic events are powerful tools, so activations are now the largest portion of B2B marketing budgets and a significant part of leading B2C brand emerging brands budgets.
8. Build brand equity first	Brand equity is what your clients say about you, and hence the key to building trust. Do great work over time and get your clients to share it on review sites such as Yelp. In-depth case studies of happy customers on the company website or shared with prospective customers builds further trust. Over time, brand equity will grow.

9. Embrace transparency	The most successful brands build trust by reducing the gap between a brand promise and its delivery. Whether through investing in data security, crowdsourcing new products from customer feedback, or implementing socially conscious practices across an entire supply chain, such tactics help leading brands deliver trust and a superior user experience.
10. Look to your audience for answers	Brands that focus on understanding their audience, what they want, and how the offer will be of value to them earn trust, so creating customer personas helps this process. This drives authentic, meaningful communications steeped reflecting the audience's worldview. Consistent application reinforces this.
11. Use proof points	Customer testimonials provide proof points of the value the brand delivers, a company and executive awards program can establish industry credibility, and well-articulated service guarantees, which eliminate risk for prospects to provide reassurance.
12. Provide value	Brand trust is earned by providing value for customers, rather than merely promoting a product or service. This can be done by posting content that is relevant to their industry and posting informative content that gives them authority in their field. This also shows customers you care about them personally, which further increases trust.

Brand Activation and Its Role in Building Trust

Brand activation is the process of making a brand well known and loved by consumers.

Brands do not become trusted by accident; when a product first enters the market, it is generally unknown to the public, until events are created that enable the public to become familiar with the brand or even to become part of the brand community. In 1962, Volvo entered the American car market as an unknown brand and successfully used customer engagement tools such as experiential events, customer participation, and memorable advertising campaigns to earn recognition as safe and robust vehicles. One of their most successful campaigns used the unconventional strapline "Drive it like you hate it" with huge success in terms of both recall and sales.

Especially in B2C markets, brand activations are a key step in creating positive perceptions; quite apart from events, tastings, samplings, in-store promotions, and merchandising and sponsorship can raise the profile of

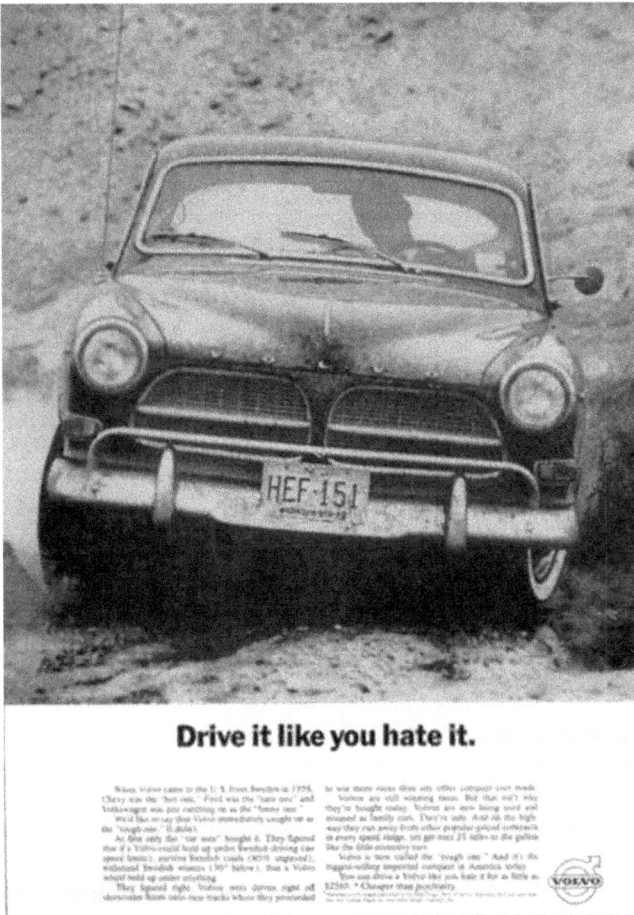

Figure 4.15 Volvo 1962 U.S. ad campaign reproduced with kind permission from Volvo

the brand, align it with desired core values, positioning it for a sustainable future. Effectively done, these activities create lasting emotional engagement and trust that delivers brand equity that helps brands endure for decades, such as Mars, the chocolate bar loved the world over since 1932.

Getting It Right: Brand Activation

Inspiring demand for a particular brand requires the organization to tap into the consumers' passions using creative strategies and ideas and go on to connect with consumers at the right time and in the right place in order to encourage them to try the brand and become loyal. Experiencing the brand in person through an experiential event can encourage consumers to recognize the brand and its values, which is an incremental step toward purchase.

Shell recently used a TV petroleum advert with pop stars to engage the younger generation, focusing on a free festival of ideas and innovation at London's Queen Elizabeth Olympic Park. It showcased bright ideas from school children, students, entrepreneurs, and industries to explore what a lower-carbon energy future might look like. The Shell Eco-marathon Europe is a centerpiece that challenges students to design and build ultra-energy-efficient cars, then drive them on a purpose-built track to see which can travel the furthest on the least amount of energy. The current record stands at 3,771km, that is, from London to Helsinki and back again on just one liter of fuel! A dedicated schools' program for Make the Future Live and website, with a Twitter feed *#make the future* offer an integrated campaign, with appeal for Shell's upcoming young consumers.

Creating Authenticity

Information provision is an essential element of trust building, especially online. Consumers need to be able to access good-quality, reliable

Figure 4.16 Excerpt from the Skittles website, accessed July 31, 2018 reproduced with kind permission from Mars Inc.

information as they move through their decision making. Brand authenticity is of particular importance to millennials, both as consumers and as employees. A Google search on *authentic marketing* yields over 17 million articles, indicating the growing interest in this area. Millennials do not like being advertised to; modern marketers need to stop selling and start engaging on customers' terms to drive pull-marketing efforts at scale. This is where authenticity comes to the fore—meaning real, genuine, of verifiable origin.

This means less talking about authenticity and more enactment of authentic behavior. Skittles brand attributes for its *Taste the rainbow* campaign were unexpected and created a clear and authentic brand perspective that engaged its audience and resulted in a lot of fun and increased sales.

When real people advocate for brands by inspiring, informing, and entertaining audiences across social, content, and video, the meaning is powerful. Your audience responds to content they want, in their language from people they trust. Paid creators, if they are to be believable, must feel a true connection to the brand and a belief in the brand, so that their message comes from the heart.

Olay, Capitol Records, and Mode produced several videos featuring Capitol Record's COO Michelle Jubelirer, a powerful female music industry executive. Michelle balances looking great, feeling great, working great, and great parenting. The video series, which featured Olay products, generated 10 million video views in two weeks, demonstrating the power of giving consumers content they love from people they trust.

When a brand can stand up for itself, rather than having to be sold, everyday people, professional creators, and experts can communicate their love for the brand in their words and style; negatives as well as positives about the brand come out, but responding to both in a constructive manner gives the opportunity not only to be authentic, but to establish a genuine relationship with customers.

Businesses that fully meet their customers' needs instill trust. Assigning reps to specific customers so that they can build a relationship helps reinforce this. VIP treatment for the best customers lets them know they are appreciated. Special services can create further opportunities for deepening the relationship. Focus groups, interviewing customers, or running a survey to get ideas can go beyond research and make the customer feel valued.

Emotional relationship	Sustainable relationship	
Harley Davidson		Apple
Volvo	Amazon	
	Toyota	
Chevrolet		
	Costco	
		Southwest airlines
Limited relationship	Reluctant relationship	
Sears		
Motorola		
KFC		
American airlines	Comcast	
	AT&T	

MARKET SHARE

TRUST

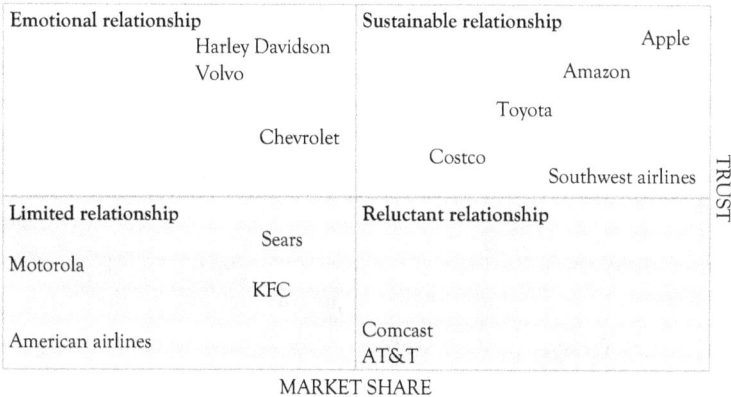

Figure 4.17 Brand sustainability map adapted from (http://adage. com/article/news/dawn-relationship-era-marketing/231792/)

Customers will feel even more valued if they feel they are important members of a community. Communities bring various customers together in numerous ways, including webinars, interactive websites, social media, trade shows, and conventions. While your customers come to these forums to learn from you, you can learn as much—if not more—from them.

Marketers should aim to create programs and processes that help fulfill the dreams and desires of audiences in ways that are in line with their normal behavior. This approach to openness is far more likely to win the hearts of millennials seeking authenticity than any heavy sales campaign. The following image shows the difference between the different types of relationships—what company would not want a sustainable relationship built on mutual trust?

Trust in an Online Environment

Online shopping increases at a faster rate than traditional shopping, but not every website visitor becomes a shopper, so converting a website visitor into a shopper is a key issue for e-merchants, just as converting footfall is in stores. Two-thirds of online shoppers say that they will not shop on a poorly designed website, and wealthy online shoppers are even less likely to do so (Chen and Teng 2013).

The online environment creates little opportunity for interaction with salespeople, so this human element of building trust is missing. Store image plays a huge role in building trust in the offline environment, and this is also a key role in creating websites, which goes beyond simple navigation of the website to all aspects of online store image. (Elliott and Speck 2005) listed six factors of online store image (ease of use, product information, entertainment, trust, customer support, and currency).

In e-commerce, loyal customers are considered extremely valuable. Loyalty is generally attributed to satisfaction with the quality of service. Because online transactions involve many uncertainties for the customer, trust is a condition for exchange. Trust in the electronic medium—*e-trust*—is believed to increase online customer loyalty, but empirical confirmations are scarce. The roles of service quality, satisfaction, and trust in an e-commerce context are key to establishing trust; research shows e-trust directly affects loyalty. The e-service quality dimension of assurance, that is, trusting the merchant, influences loyalty via e-trust and e-satisfaction. Other e-quality dimensions, such as ease of use, e-scape, responsiveness, and customization, influence e-loyalty mainly indirectly, via satisfaction.

Trust indicates that an online shopper perceives a level of reliability, safety, and trustworthiness in the online store brand. A website that is easy to use can increase trust in the online store brand when online shoppers recognize that the online store brand is willing to make investment

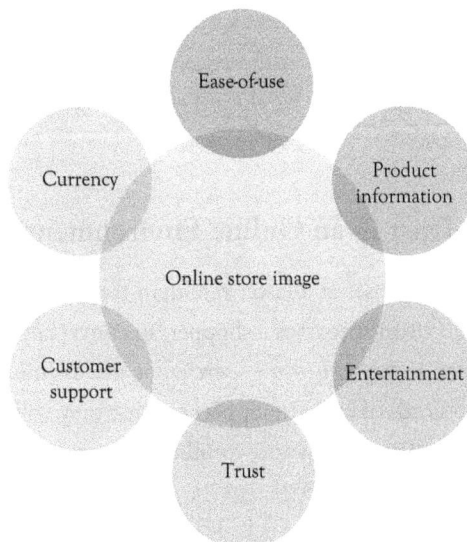

Figure 4.18 Aspects of online store image adapted from (Elliot and Speck 2005)

in building its exchange relationship with them. Online shoppers engage with online stores mainly through the website interface, so the character of the website is a demonstration of the brand personality. A straightforward website that explains the process can create trust and reduce misunderstandings. In a physical retail store, the customer forms trust on his or her perception of the salesperson, and he or she is more likely to trust a physical retail store when he or she feels that the salesperson is easy to communicate with; the quality of contact and communication with the salesperson has an effect on trust. Open communication between two parties fosters an easy exchange of information, leading to increased understanding and trust. An online shopper is likely to have more trust in an online store brand if he or she perceives the website as easy to use, indicating that the online store brand operates in good faith. Investment in a website's ease of use provides evidence that the online store owner's motives are benevolent and can be trusted. Conversely, an impenetrable website might imply that the online store owner is being dishonest or is hiding something through an unnecessarily complicated interface, thereby decreasing the perception of trust.

Whether the online shoppers achieve their expected usefulness from the website interface not only depends on the technology itself, but also on the extent of the human service behind the website. Trust is particularly important when the social exchange involves risk or uncertainty, as is the case with online shopping. Fears may lie around whether goods are actually dispatched, or around the quality of what is purchased, or value for money. Trust refers to subjective guarantees that the online store brand can meet its obligations, will behave as promised, and genuinely care about its customers. When an online store brand can be trusted, online shoppers perceive usefulness by receiving the increased benefits, that is, gaining useful information from the website and accomplishing their tasks successfully as expected.

Familiarity is often based on advertising exposure; a common assumption is that a well-known company can better serve them and support their desires. Advertising exposure generally requires the use of third parties, and large companies have more resources to make this investment. A larger online store may also have superior procedures that enable it to operate more effectively.

For an online retailer, this may include choice in delivery options, accuracy of delivery, and speed of delivery for the products and services offered through the online store. In online environments, the more difficult it is for consumers to assess product (or delivery) performance prior to purchase with complete information, the more likely consumers are to rely on familiarity of online stores to form expectations or to evaluate the ability of the online store to supply and deliver quality products in a timely manner. Simple website interfaces enable online shoppers to more easily search for useful information, which improves their perception of usefulness and makes them more likely to buy.

When Things Go Wrong: Service Recovery

Customers are generally reasonable people, who accept that things can go wrong in service provision. Such occurrences present a major opportunity for organizations to demonstrate their trustworthiness. When a customer raises an issue with the customer support team or any member of the frontline team, there is a major chance for the organization to strengthen the relationship and to delight the customer. This is discussed in greater depth in the Chapter 5, but it is important to understand how to deal with this from the trust perspective.

The key to building trust in the situation is to listen attentively to what the customer has to say, not to lay or to accept blame, but acknowledge how the customer feels up. Understanding what the customer would ideally like to happen and attempting to deliver it or better still exceeded it help make the customer feel that the organization has their best interests at heart. This allows any tension in this situation to defuse, leaves the customer satisfied and likely to return, and to recommend the organization to others.

Quotations or Interviews from Key Practitioners and Leaders of Excellence Businesses

If people like you, they'll listen to you, but if they trust you, they'll do business with you.
—Zig Ziglar (American author, salesman and motivational speaker)

When you form a team, why do you try to form the team? Because teamwork builds trust and trust builds speed.
—Russell Honore (retired Lieutenant General who served as the 33rd commanding general of the U.S. First Army at Fort Gillem, Georgia)

It takes 20 years to build a reputation and five minutes to ruin it.
—Warren Buffett

If you don't have trust inside your company, then you can't transfer it to your customers.
—Roger Staubach (American football quarterback)

Trust is the lubrication that makes it possible for organizations to work.
—Warren Bennis (American scholar and consultant)

Trust is like an eraser–it gets smaller and smaller (after every mistake)
Anon

"To give real service you must add something which cannot be bought or measured with money, and that is sincerity and integrity."
–Douglas Adams

It takes twenty years to build a reputation and only five minutes to ruin it. If you think about that you'll do things differently.
–Warren Buffet

End of Chapter Summary

This chapter has explored the components of trust and its role in customer relationship marketing into the future, as customers become more involved in the development, production, and feedback of services, as well as marketing communications around services.

It has considered how business processes support trust in the relationship and deliver the brand promise. It discusses the 1:10:100 rule and how organizations can anticipate critical incidents and deal with unexpected events to create trust and delight.

It challenges companies to ask for feedback, deal with it constructively, rather than being defensive about it—own it and do something with it. Managing positive and negative comments effectively can move a relationship from transactional to deep loyalty and advocacy. This aspect of dealing with customer concerns also links to the *Be there* element of the FISH! Principles.

End of Chapter Review Questions

Organizational Trust: Internal

	Strongly agree	Agree	Neither agree nor disagree	Disagree	Strongly disagree
If I have a problem at work, I know my co-workers will try to help me out					
The people I work with will pull together to get the job done					
Most of my co-workers can be relied on to do as they say they will do					
The management of this organization tries to understand the workers' point of view					
I feel that my co-workers and I will be treated fairly					
The management of this organization would be willing to deceive employees if they thought it would give them an advantage					
I have confidence in the abilities of my co-workers					

Most of my co-workers would get the job done even if the boss were not around to check					
Other workers make my job more difficult by careless work					
Our organization has a poor future unless it can attract better managers					
The management of this organization makes decisions that will be good for the future					
My supervisor is competent					
The managers in this organization cooperate to get the work done					
The managers of this organization help everyone to understand what needs to be done					
This organization shows its concerns for its customers by giving them high-quality products and service					
This organization is out to make a quick buck or get by					

Source: Stefan Veronescu (2015).

Organizational Trust: Customers

Question	Strongly agree	Agree	Neither agree nor disagree	Disagree	Strongly disagree
Our staff convey empathy, patience, and consistency					
Our staff are adaptable and can handle surprises, negative or positive constructively					
Our staff communicate clearly, using authentically positive language					
Our staff stay focused on their task, have a strong work ethic, see problems through to the conclusion					
Our staff are well informed about our products and services and not afraid to refer unusual queries to management					
Our staff are willing to accept responsibility for their own actions					
Our staff respond positively to feedback					
Our customers receive a consistent response at all of our touchpoints					
We provide opportunities for our customers to give feedback on our service					
As an organization, we welcome customer feedback and act on it					

Our customers can easily contact people in our organization if they have a problem or query					
We reinforce relation-ship-building with customers wherever possible					
We actively offer opportunities to wel-come customers into our community					

We have a clear understanding of our customers' implicit expectations. An implicit expectation might be relative "Compared with other companies..." or "Compared to the leading brand..."					
We have a clear understanding of per-formance expectations related to the quality of outcome (may include the evaluation of accessibility, cus-tomization, depend-ability, timeliness, accuracy, and user-friendly interfaces)					
We understand cus-tomer expectations of dynamic performance (how the product or service is expected to evolve over time—the changes in support, product, or service needed to meet future business or use envi-ronments)					

We understand customer expectations of technology performance (not just feature-based, but technology that enhance perceptions of status, ego, self-image)					
We understand interpersonal customer expectations that reflect the relationship between the customer and product or service provider					
We understand how situations alter customer expectations (purchase stages, purpose of purchase, and so on)					
We actively look for opportunities to delight our customers					
Our frontline staff are empowered to deal with service recovery issues, even if it means they have to bend the rules					

Adapted from Smith, S 2018: Types of customer expectations.

References

trustbarometermediadeckuk-noembargo-150119150712-conversion-gate02.pdf

http://adage.com/article/news/dawn-relationship-era-marketing/231792/

Basu. C. 2009. Personality Not Included: Why Companies Lose Their Authenticity and How Great Brands Get it Back.

Chen, M.Y., and C.I. Teng. 2013. "A Comprehensive Model of the Effects of Online Store Image on Purchase Intention in an E-commerce Environment." *Electronic Commerce Research* 13, no. 1, 1–23. doi: https://doi-org.ezphost. dur.ac.uk/10.1007/s10660-013-9104-5

Elliott, M.T., and P.S. *Speck*. 2005. "Factors that Affect Attitude Toward a Retail Website." *Journal of Marketing Theory and Practice* 13, no. 1, pp. 40–51.

Halliburton, C., and A. Menara. 2010. *ESCP Trust and Consumer White Paper.*

Hammond, S.A., and A. Mayfield. 2004. *The Thin Book of Naming Elephants: How to Surface Undiscussables for Greater Organisational Success.* Thin Book Publishing.

https://hbr.org/2003/02/the-enemies-of-trust

https://forbes.com/sites/forbesagencycouncil/2016/09/19/12-ways-new-companies-can-build-brand-trust/2/#434efa95416d

https://link-springer-com.ezphost.dur.ac.uk/article/10.1007%2Fs10551-012-1216-7

https://issuu.com/shoppercentric/docs/wo30_sst2018?e=23309330/58125242

https://econsultancy.com/blog/66013-brand-activation-and-its-role-in-driving-consumer-engagement-and-awareness

https://s3.amazonaws.com/academia.edu.documents/31539856/3_Comfort_your.pdf?AWSAccessKeyId=AKIAIWOWYYGZ2Y53UL3A&Expires=1518458908&Signature=DwHMJfnGyphLD0RtD3JakEN4s3Y%3D&response-content-disposition=inline%3B%20filename%3D3_Comfort_your.pdf

http://mintel.com/blog/consumer-market-news/the-truth-about-trust-strengthening-consumer-trust

http://adage.com/article/digitalnext/brand-authenticity-real/303191/

https://bigthink.com/ron-day/fear-and-confidence-on-the-job-search-trail

CHAPTER 5

Exceeding Customer Needs and Expectations

Chapter Objectives

- To understand the importance of customer needs and the sources of customer satisfaction
- To understand how businesses can exceed customer expectations
- To appreciate how to manage diverse target groups with a focused marketing mix
- To appreciate the key role played by staff in delighting customers
- To identify how innovation can help you continue to engage and delight customers
- To make recommendations to exceed customers' base expectations
- To appreciate the shift toward experiences as purchases

Chapter Profile

This chapter explores why customer needs are paramount and discusses customer needs versus customer desires—what do customers really want? It looks at customer expectations and satisfaction. How should organizations manage customers when things go wrong—what are the effects of fade or walk away versus active strategies that re-engage customers back into the fold?

Planning a customer mix is also a key ingredient in delivering delight for all your target groups. Services are often delivered in an environment that involves more than one customer, so appreciating how to manage the various needs of different customer segments helps the business to maximize the customer experience, as well as its profits.

Understanding customer expectations is the key to establishing satisfaction, delight, and moving into building loyalty. Innovation can help businesses continue to engage and delight customers. Selecting staff with the right mix of attitude, skills, and desire to please all reward customers is a key part of exceeding expectations. Lastly, businesses need to manage the customer element in expectations so that they have a clear concept of their role in service delivery.

Key Terms

Servant Leadership

Total Quality Management (TQM)

Customer mix describes the array of people of differing knowledge or experience, ethnicity, and so on, who patronize a service organization. It can be narrow or broad, depending on how diverse it is.

The Importance of Understanding Customer Needs

Outstanding customer care involves getting to know your customers so well that you can anticipate their needs and exceed their expectations. For that level of understanding, you need to be attentive to customers whenever you are in contact with them. Quite apart from enabling you to deliver customer satisfaction, the rewards are great, better understanding can generate loyalty, and is new business as a result of positive word-of-mouth.

The three main ways of understand your customers better are:

- Put yourself in their shoes and look at your organization from their perspective;
- Collect and analyze data to gain insights to their buying behavior;
- Ask them what they think.

Understanding customer expectations is the key to establishing satisfaction, delight, and moving into building loyalty. Chapter 3 covered the gaps model, which explains how customer satisfaction is derived, and areas for dissatisfaction. Beyond that, ensuring that the organization has a clear understanding of customer needs is the starting point for being able to exceed expectations. Establishing a clear customer persona, outlining what life in their world is like, and possible pains or gains are important parts of the process.

When the organization and its staff understand who the main customer groups are, what market they are part of, how the product or service meets their needs, they are then well-placed to be able to meet those needs. Exceeding them then becomes a question of providing service above and beyond the expectation, and understanding what might further help customers—perhaps as a one off, or perhaps as a part of service innovation.

People are driven by aspirations, but these are hard to interpret, and go well beyond their basic needs. The customer persona information can provide useful insights here. Customers are rarely fully aware of their aspirations, but their service provider should be. Creating a mutually beneficial partnership where both the buyer and seller benefit will produce a sustainable relationship, where both parties win.

Customers are not homogenous, so it is critical that companies are able to respond flexibly to different customer types and behavior that fall outside the predictions. The art of good business is to achieve a high level of effectiveness (doing the right things) with efficiency (doing things the right way) so that you can deliver the right service for the customer while remaining cost-effective. Whatever your proposition or service, customers will always expect a measure of customer service. Even when services are completely automated, customers expect to have a *real person* on hand for assistance, if required.

Contrary to expectations, a recent BBC article discussed how a certain group of customers enjoy rude and abrasive service; one Liverpool hotel showed a rise of 20 percent in bookings following a documentary covering its unpleasant staff. Without that clear understanding of what the customer needs or wants, even if it seems counterintuitive, satisfying their expectations is really just a shot in the dark.

How to Exceed Customer Expectations

Customer expectations are difficult to meet. The higher they are, the more unlikely it is that a business will exceed them. Yet, businesses do exceed

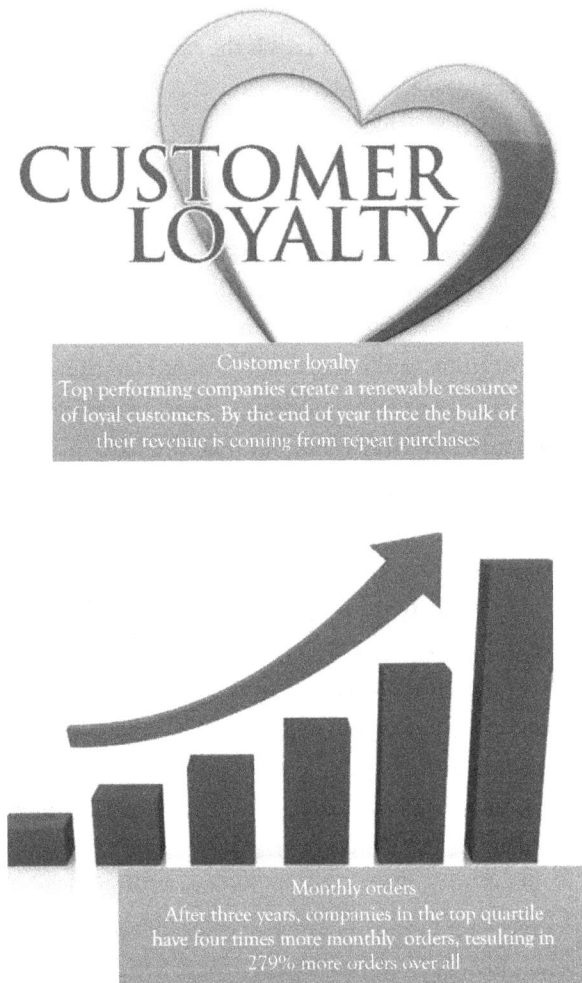

Figure 5.1 The importance of exceeding expectations and delivering profitability reproduced with kind permission from (https://rjmetrics. com/resources/reports/2015-ecommerce-growth-benchmark)

them, and there is a strong business case for doing so. It is relatively easy to do; we live in a world of mediocrity, so standing out is easy and has the ability to produce big results.

Exceeding customer expectations creates a positive association that further builds your brand and attracts customer loyalty, boosting repeat purchases and increasing your customer lifetime value (CLV), an important metric for ecommerce businesses. In fact, the most successful e-commerce businesses make the majority of their revenues from repeat purchases past year three of operation. A customer with a good experience will tell others, helping you acquire new customers and lowering your overall marketing acquisition costs.

When you exceed customer expectations, you create customers who spend more money, purchase more frequently, and help you acquire more customers by sharing their experience. *In all three ways that an ecommerce business can make more revenue, overdelivering on expectations helps you achieve it.*

Research shows 80 percent of the companies believe they are providing superior customer service, while only 8 percent of their clients agree with them. With such different perceptions of quality achievement, clearly there is a disconnect between what customers understand as good service and what organizations understand by the term.

The three areas most important to customers, and therefore the easiest for exceeding expectations are:

Quality First, Speed Second

RightNow's customer experience impact study cites the top reason (82 percent) customers would stop using a business was rude and incompetent staff. This was 18 percent more than not having their issue resolved swiftly.

However, most businesses use speed as their main measure of customer service quality.

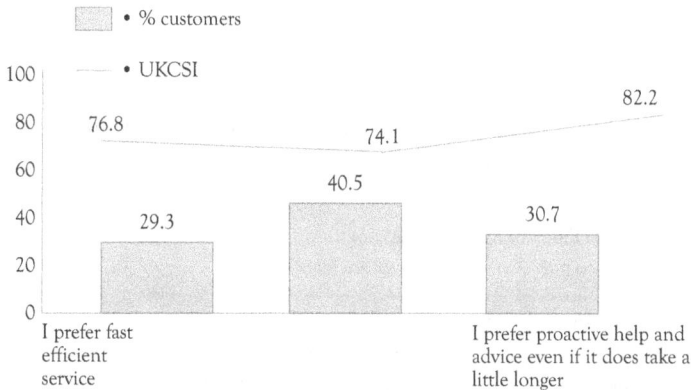

Figure 5.2 Customer service preferences reproduced with kind permission from The Institute of Customer Service UK

United Airlines bucked this trend for Kerry Drake, traveling to see his mother in her final hours. His first flight was delayed, but stewards on board realized his distress, the captain radioed ahead to hold his connecting flight ensuring that he could spend a few hours with his mother before she died. This makes for memorable service. When time is not the only measure of quality, your people can concentrate on getting your service right. A rushed customer is never a happy one.

Connect with Your Customers

It is no longer enough to be friendly and efficient in solving customer inquiries. You have to connect with them too. This is hard to do in an authentic manner, but the best approach is to allow staff to be themselves, rather than use a prescribed script. As you will have recruited staff with the right kind of attitude, and managed to feel empowered to deliver outstanding service, this come over as authenticity, rather than the ubiquitous "Have a nice day."

Connecting with customers when you communicate through e-mail or webchat is much harder, because it lacks the dimensions of tone of voice and body language. The following conversation is from a webchat between Jill, a representative for online men's clothing store Jack Threads, and a man who had found a hole in a shirt he had bought from them. He had not yet worn the shirt as he was hoping to lose some weight. Jill firstly congratulated the client on losing weight, before asking for more information to help him return the shirt. The customer, Tony, then went on to explain he was training for a marathon. This conversation went viral, despite its apparent simplicity—companies are so fixated on solving customer queries, they forget to connect with them. This illustrates that giving your employees more freedom makes them happier and more likely to connect with clients.

> Tony: I'm training for a marathon.
> Jill: no prob-i'm setting up a return for you now
> Jill: Nice!!!
> Jill: When is that?
> Tony: In October. It would be my first one, so i'm preparing now. Lol
> Jill: Good for you! I did a half marathon last October and woo i am so impressed by ppl who can do a full!

Figure 5.3 Jack Thread's webchat conversation

Go the Extra Mile

There is a lot of talk in customer service circles about *going the extra mile*; what it really boils down to is doing something above and beyond what you promise and giving customers something memorable. This is often achieved by a frontline member of staff taking the initiative and doing far more than was expected of them.

A family staying at the Ritz-Carlton, Bali, had brought specialized eggs and milk for their son who suffered from food allergies. Upon arrival, the eggs had broken and the milk had soured. The Ritz-Carlton manager and dining staff searched the town, but could not find the appropriate items. However, the executive chef remembered a store in Singapore that sold them. He contacted his mother-in-law and asked her to buy the products and fly to Bali to deliver them, which she did.

From time to time, a customer will give you the opportunity to provide them with a really memorable service. A young Ritz customer left his beloved toy Joshie the Giraffe at the hotel; his father's explanation was that he had stayed on vacation a little longer. The father Chris Hurn e-mailed the Ritz to explain the situation. They responded by not only sending the beloved toy home, but by creating a photo booklet showing everything Joshie had done during his extra stay.

This approach keeps regular customers loyal and makes your business the one they recommend to friends and family.

Map Out Touchpoints

The customer touchpoints are a key element in ensuring that the customer has a consistent brand message and also spotting opportunities for improving the customer experience. The starting point is to map all the touchpoints by breaking your visitor experience into categories and listing all the touchpoints within each category.

There are various approaches, including considering the access points to the organization, such as e-mail, telephone, and social media. Using stages in the purchasing process is a useful way to break things down:

- Prepurchase: All the interactions a visitor or customer has with your brand prior to purchase.

- Purchase: The interactions a customer has while purchasing from you.
- Postpurchase: All the interactions a customer has with you after purchasing from your brand.

The next step is to identify each touchpoint within each stage:

Prepurchase	During purchase	Postpurchase
Social media	Product photos	Purchase receipt
Live chat	Product descriptions	Received package
Advertising or marketing	Contact page	Thank you note
E-mail enquires	Checkout experience	Return policy

The Role of Staff in Exceeding Customer Expectations

Business owners need self-motivated staff with initiative who can get the job done, because employee performance is critical to the overall success of the company. Recruiting staff with the right kind of attitude is more important than finding people with the required skillset. Skills can be trained, while attitude is more a part of character. Understanding the key elements of employee performance enables business owners to develop consistent and objective methods for evaluating employees. This helps determine strengths, weaknesses, and potential managerial gaps in the business organization. Performance evaluations are never fun, but they do help business leaders determine performance levels for each employee.

One of the most important factors in employee performance is goal achievement. Successful employees meet deadlines, make sales, and build the brand through positive customer interactions. When employees do not perform effectively, consumers feel that the company is neglectful toward them and will shift to an alternative supplier. Effective employees get things done properly the first time. If the internal customer reports person is always late producing them, the client services department cannot carry out their role, look unprofessional, and even incompetent.

The following chart shows that, of the top four differentiators for high-performing organizations, three relate to staff in the organization. Staff are the people who enact customer service, so this makes sense—even the fourth factor is dependent on the quality of staff involved.

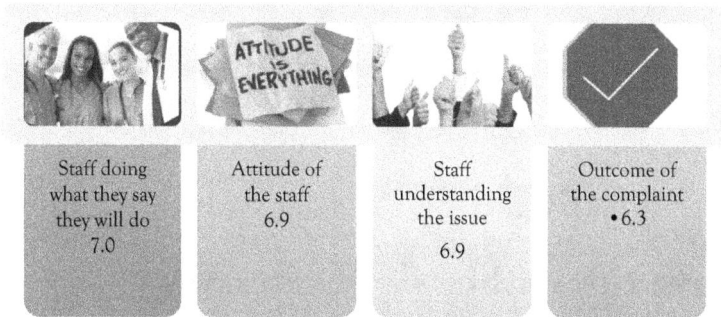

| Staff doing what they say they will do 7.0 | Attitude of the staff 6.9 | Staff understanding the issue 6.9 | Outcome of the complaint • 6.3 |

Figure 5.4 The top four differentiators for high-scoring organizations adapted from the Institute of Customer Service

Positive Work Environment

Positive people, working at their roles effectively and with positivity, generate a positive environment, everyone is happier and more motivated, and morale is high. The reverse is equally true—one negative person can bring the whole department down; it is important to foster a positive, energetic work environment. A positive work environment that rewards high performers with incentives and group recognition boosts performance overall and attracts quality talent, because the office feels vibrant and successful. Providing what your team needs, both in resources and managerial support, can tailor a creative and productive work environment. There has been much discussion about the differences between the expectations of millennials and other groups of workers and the need to cater for these in designing the work experience. By 2020, millennials well account for 70 percent of the total workforce, so meeting their needs will be an important element in success for the future. Having them in the workforce will help ensure that the organization can keep its service offering relevant for the marketplace.

Measure Employee Growth

Employee evaluation enables the management and team members to see their growth and how to make progress over time. It provides new goals, keeping the office energy high. Rewards encourage high-performing employees to exceed their efforts in successive periods, ensuring that the organization is cultivating its strength to grow into something bigger to

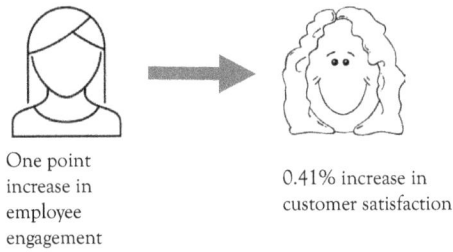

One point
increase in
employee
engagement

0.41% increase in
customer satisfaction

*Figure 5.5 The contribution engaged employees make to customer
satisfaction adapted from the Institute of Customer Service*

the benefit of the entire organization. Watching employees grow reveals
managerial potential, and internal promotions create a healthy competition and attracts more high-caliber staff.

A weak manager can often make the mistake of thinking that poor
performance indicates a poor employee. Underperforming employees
negatively affect productivity and ultimately, the bottom line. Team performance is mostly the domain of the manager; by seeking common trends
in employees who are succeeding and those where there are deficiencies,
smart managers can evaluate whether deficiencies are talent issues or management and development issues. This can inform team training strategies
and future recruiting strategies.

Ultimately, good employees are productive, which creates great working environments and increases overall productivity. Evaluations help
establish how to encourage employees to grow so that they can excel.

The Role of the Leader

All leaders talk about the importance of engaging others in the vision,
but outstanding leaders convey depth and higher purpose when speaking
about vision, seeing it as a clarion call for employees' commitment and
engagement. Strong leaders use vision to align people through a cascade
of objectives, creating strong functional integration across the organization, rather than a silo mentality.

Most leaders appreciate the need for trust, respect, and honesty in
motivating their teams. Exceptional leaders understand how to orchestrate team members to create the conditions for exceptional performance,
as well as their own role in creating a motivating work environment.

Good → **Outstanding**

Good	Outstanding
Objectives and targets	People and engagement
Act due to beliefs and values	Act due to consequences
Focus on skill	Focus on attitude and engagement
Delegate tasks	Delegate space for autonomy
Believe leader holds responsibility	Wants team to own
Involvement in the vision and strategy	Cocreation of vision and strategy
Give time to others	Focus on people as route to success
Tend to focus on work	Seek to understand people and motives
Vision as clarity of purpose	Vision as emotional clarion call
Focus on team structure and location	Focus on team cohesion and equality
Give a good impression	Reflect on symbolic role of leadership
Reflect on learning about job	Reflect on learning about self and others
People and task important	People at centre-task through people
WYSIWYG (what you see is what you get)	Consistent and careful on behavior
Development through learning and coaching	Developed through challenge and support
Use systems and procedures	Focus on a few key procedures reduce burden
Attend to many things	People first then move on

Figure 5.6 The difference between good and great

Consistency is crucial, and leaders must control their emotions, and not betray any misgivings they may feel.

In response to failure, outstanding leaders try to maintain and build trust, focusing on achievements and garnering a learning experience from the situation. An absence of failure suggests a lack of creativity and innovation, and the organization is, therefore, unlikely to achieve peak performance.

Team spirit and engagement are fundamental to success, and outstanding leaders manage team bonding, form deep relationships, and cocreate plans to achieve this, rather than making a decision and handing out tasks.

Great leaders see people as the route to performance: they are deeply invested in people and relationships, not just people-oriented attention. For outstanding leaders, people are the only route to sustainable performance; they understand at a deep level that exceptional performance is only achieved through the capability and engagement of people. They do not simply surrender control to others, rather, they facilitate and nurture empowerment through conscious philosophy and practice.

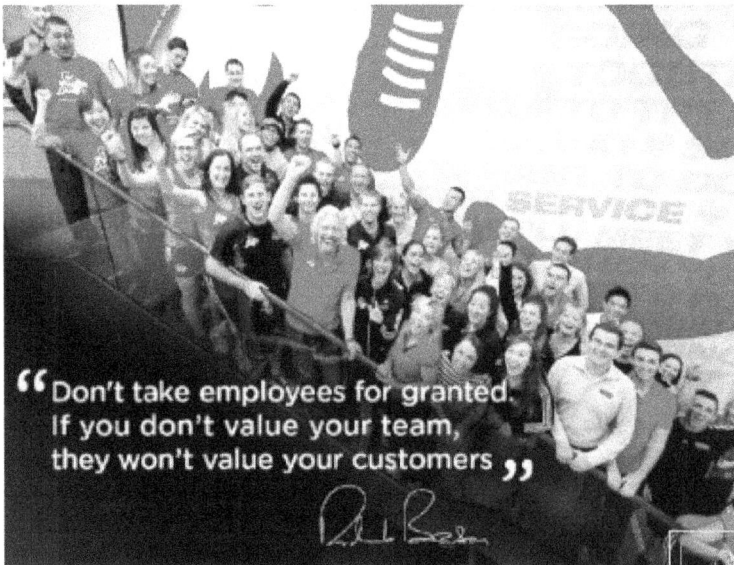

Figure 5.7 The Virgin perspective on employees quotation reproduced with kind permission from virgin.com

Servant leadership, an idea originating from Robert Greenleaf in the United States during the 1960s, has been revived by a number of organizations in recent years, placing emphasis on the leader as serving the people. Outstanding leaders understand excellent performance depends on people; their role is to engage others in the endeavor, so a common purpose and goal provide unified motivation. The best leaders focus on the outcome as the purpose and align their team to this.

Outstanding leaders see their own positivity as important, but recognize that consistency and creating unified purpose are more so. They speak about seeing the whole, using sophisticated processes to create excellence, and about harnessing capability and autonomy of people to deliver. They recognize that how they are with people hinders or helps the team to support the vision.

The Role of Process

Aside from exceptional people and leaders, processes make a huge contribution to achieving superlative service. There is a strong link between behavior and outcomes, and systems can provide clarity on what needs to be done.

Viewing the organization holistically, rather than compartmentalizing, enables the parts to be connected by a guiding sense of purpose, identifying how action follows reaction, how culture is created by events. Clear processes create confidence that acts as a springboard to motivation and creativity, allowing trust in all links in the chain to speed interactions and enable people to take personal risks and succeed.

TQM seeks to improve quality and performance to meet or exceed customer expectations by integrating all quality-related functions and processes across the organization. It looks at the overall quality measures in an organization, including design and development, quality control and maintenance, quality improvement, and quality assurance. It reviews all quality measures at all levels from all company employees.

TQM can be defined as the management of initiatives and procedures that are aimed at achieving the delivery of quality products and services. A number of key principles can be identified in defining TQM, including:

- Executive management: Management acts as the main driver for TQM, creating an environment that ensures its success.
- Training: Employees receive regular training on the methods and concepts of quality.
- Customer focus: Improvements in quality improve customer satisfaction.
- Decision making: Quality decisions are made based on measurements.
- Methodology and tools: Appropriate methodology and tools ensure that nonconformance incidents are identified, measured, and responded to consistently.
- Continuous improvement: Companies should continuously work toward improving manufacturing and quality procedures.
- Company culture: The culture of the company focuses on employees' ability to collaborate to improve quality.
- Employee involvement: Employees are encouraged to be proactive in identifying and addressing quality-related problems.

The following chart shows a comparison between top performing organizations and the rest relating to the ease of contact over the telephone. Success demonstrated by a metric of this nature is achieved by a combination of sound leadership, effective processes, and exceptional people.

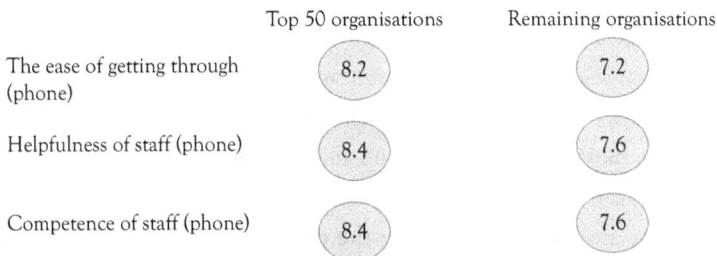

	Top 50 organisations	Remaining organisations
The ease of getting through (phone)	8.2	7.2
Helpfulness of staff (phone)	8.4	7.6
Competence of staff (phone)	8.4	7.6

Figure 5.8 Ease and effectiveness of telephone communication adapted from The Institute of Customer Service

Managing the Customer Mix

The term *customer mix* describes the array of people of differing knowledge or experience, ethnicity, and so on, who patronize a service organization. It can be narrow or broad, depending on how diverse it is.

Customers can enhance or undermine other customers' service experience. Customer-to-customer interactions (CCI) are often challenged by crowding, lengthy queues and waiting times, and broad customer mix. Lack of organizational oversight into these factors can lead to a high level of discomfort, or even distress for customers, and must, therefore, form part of the planning process so that every customer has a positive experience. Organizations should work hard to create positive CCI and minimize negative ones.

Customer-to-employee interactions (CEI) can be friendly interactions—the optimal interaction for organizations and customers. On occasion, however, unfriendly interactions can be highly disruptive and have negative effects on the service experience and on staff morale. Excessively friendly interactions may delay the service, embarrass other customer and staff. The latter two CEI situations should be covered as part of employees' social skills training.

Significant differences in individuals' evaluations of other customers' behaviors are often rooted in easily observable characteristics. Some customers have a tendency to be less inhibited when they are out of town or among strangers, hence the concept of *Brits abroad* when young people overindulge in alcohol and feel that they own the country they are visiting on holiday and behave in a manner that others find unpleasant.

Service organizations that attract a diverse customer base should address some customers' tendency to criticize other groups and attempt to encourage random acts of kindness among customers. Selecting an

Table 5.1 Issues around the customer mix adapted from Fodor's Travel publications Internet survey (1999)

1	The smelly passenger	39.5%
2	The baby or small child	19.0%
3	Overweight person who spills over the armrest	17.3%
4	The talker who won't shut up	12.4%

appropriate customer mix can encourage positive customer-to-customer relationships when customers are likely to interact, yet have different backgrounds or reasons for using the service.

Customer rage: Mild to extreme anger about some aspect of the service experience may be prompted by workers, other customers, the setting, or the process. It can distress workers and/or customers, cause costly damage to the servicescape, disruption of service delivery, negative publicity, legal action, and so on, so it is important that service staff are trained to deal effectively with it.

Other customers are a component of most service experiences and are captured in audience (service theater model), which compares service delivery to a theater performance, as they share several parallel characteristics. Both need a good performance to impress the audience or customers, both require careful planning and execution at back end, and proper stage setting for dramatic effect. Service involves theatrical elements just as a stage production does: audience, actors, setting, backstage, front stage, and performance or delivery.

Service Theater Framework

Audience: Customers who consume services.

Actors: Service providers who create service experience for audience (customers).

Setting: Service environment (servicescape) where service delivery takes place.

Backstage: Backstage actions are not visible to audience (customers), but may involve planning and execution of activities.

The Servuction Model (Hoffman and Bateson 2011)

This model covers factors that influence service experience, both visible and invisible to customers. The invisible component is mainly systems, regulations, and processes by which the organization functions. Although invisible to customers, they form an essential part of the service experience.

The visible part comprises: servicescape, contact personnel, service providers, and other consumers.

Servicescape: It refers to the service environment, including ambient conditions such as music, scenery, props, and other aspects that form a backdrop to the service experience, as well as business equipment and furniture used in delivering the service.

Contact personnel: Employees other than primary providers that interact with consumer, such as a receptionist.

Service provider: This is the primary service operative, such as a hairdresser, doctor, dentist, or instructor.

Customers: Customer A is the recipient of the benefits created by the service experience. Customer B: All other customers who are part of Customer A's experience.

This model recognizes other customers are an integral part of service process. The level of participation may be active or passive, but they are present. Service designers must account for the interactive nature of services and customer involvement in the production process. All elements of the servuction model combine to create the experience for the customer.

Managing the Customer Element in Service Provision

If customers are to play their role effectively in the service experience, service providers need to *select* them, using appropriate segmentation, and then *train* them so that their role is clear.

Customer Training Guidelines

Achieving satisfaction across all customer groups with the same service delivery is virtually impossible. Effective customer persona mapping can help identify groups of customers with similar needs so that service performance can be standardized to some degree.

In addition to managing issues arising from a broad customer mix, service organizations can devise methods for improving customer-to-customer relationships and encourage random acts of kindness as part of their role within the service delivery process.

Customer scripts can help customers navigate the servicescape and the service process effectively; good signage and timely announcements can ensure that customers are in the right place at the right time, for example, doctors' surgeries usually call out the name of the next patient and the room they need to go to.

The Experience Economy and Its Role in Service Excellence

Western economies have gone through an evolution over many centuries: they began as raw material and agriculture economies (primary), moving into manufacturing (secondary), and then service (tertiary). The latest evolution has seen something of a split between information and experience. The term *experience economy* first appeared in a 1998 article by B. Joseph Pine and James H. Gilmore. They analyzed consumer economic trends and observed that consumers were increasingly gravitating toward purchase behavior dictated by the quality of the experience in addition to the quality of the service or good itself.

They suggest that businesses must orchestrate memorable events for their customers, and that memory itself becomes the product: the

Usability	A piece of equipment that is pleasant to handle commands a higher price and enjoys higher sales volumes than competitors with similar functionality but less hand appeal.
Customer service	A restaurant that welcomes customers with friendly and prompt service builds a loyal base of customers, and even on quiet week nights, attracts plenty of people while competitors are quiet.
Luxury	Customers are willing to pay a premium for the pleasure of being in an iconic building, or one that has been fitted out to a very high standard. Such destinations rarely have vacancies, despite the costs.
Status	Branded items are seen as status symbols, giving access to groups, and denoting wealth. Followers of celebrities often choose their clothes and accessories based on their hero's choice.
Culture	As people have more disposable income, they seek new food tastes and new forms of music and entertainment.
Well-being	Products and services that provide a sense of well-being such as a relaxing spa.
Peak experiences	Customers view some experiences, such as a wedding or holiday, as accomplishments that are important to their life.
Transformative experiences	Experiences that transform an individual to make them better such as education or an inspiring book.

experience, echoing some of the concepts of service as drama, and the servuction model (Hoffman and Bateson 1987). Some experience businesses charge for the transformation that the customer undergoes as a result of the experience. Education, such as an MBA, is a classic example of this, but more recently, spiritual offerings are also entering into this arena. The concept of the experience economy is particularly important in retail, tourism, and it is also permeating health care provision, and as a consequence, is a key consideration for architecture and urban planning.

Within a service environment, an appreciation of the experience economy is one of the underpinning of customer experience management. It is based on the idea that products and services can differentiate by creating an experience that customers value. When many products and services have become commodities, experience offers an inimitable means of distinction. There are eight dimensions of how experience can add value to products and services:

Customer Element in Expectations

Some level of customer participation is required in service delivery. Services are *performances*, usually produced and consumed simultaneously. Often, employees, customers, and other people in the service environment combine to create the ultimate service outcome. Each customer participates in the service delivery process and can enhance or destroy it for others through appropriate or inappropriate, effective or ineffective, productive or unproductive behaviors.

In a classroom or in a training situation, students (customers) interact with the instructor and other students as they consume the educational services. As these customers are all present during the service production, they may contribute to or detract from the successful delivery of the service and to their own satisfaction.

Customers who are uncertain what they want to order can take an enormous amount of staff time, as they decide, and when they are not ready with payment, they slow down checkout operators. These distractions leave other customers and calls unattended, causing longer wait times and dissatisfaction; providing clear cues can smooth these issues.

Some services require a high level of customer participation; others are much lower. Often, the customer's physical presence (low level of participation) is all that is needed, and employees perform all of the service production work, as in the case of a musical concert, where listeners must be present to receive the entertainment service. In other cases, consumer inputs aid the service organization in creating the service delivery (moderate level of participation). For a service such as tailored training, the client needs to provide a considerable amount of information regarding their objectives, the nature of the individuals to be trained, the amount of time available, and maybe, the use of premises for delivery. Customer inputs can include *information, effort, or physical possessions.* Consulting and training engagements usually have high customer involvement as they co create the service.

Customer's Roles

Service customers can be seen as *partial employees*, as they contribute to the organization's productive capacity.

Customer inputs can impact the organization's productivity, either through quality or quantity—for example, in a consulting context:

- Clients who clearly articulate the solution they desire.
- Provide needed information in a timely manner.
- Communicate openly.
- Gain the commitment of key internal stakeholders.
- Raise issues during the process in a timely way will get better service.

Customers also make a major contribution to their own satisfaction, as well as the quality of the services they receive. Adding to the productivity of an organization is unlikely to motivate customers, but they are likely to care whether their own needs are met. Effective signposting and scripting can increase success of service delivery and ensure that customer needs are met. Many personal services, such as dental care, education, fitness, and weight management, are highly dependent on customers following directions; when they fail to do this, they do not get the desired outcomes. In an educational setting, interactive learning, as opposed to passive listening, not only increases learning outcomes, but produces much greater satisfaction.

Many of the services customers buy are ones they could perform for themselves, such as home decorating or cleaning, so in this sense, they can also be viewed as a potential competitor. On a regular basis, customers have to decide whether they should pay for service (*external exchange*) or perform it for themselves (*internal exchange*). Organization make similar internal versus external exchange decisions that may end up as outsourcing functions such as recruitment, accountancy, and payroll. This decision allows them to focus on their core activities and employ experts to deal with more generic functional areas. Decisions around outsourcing are often financially informed, but also go through fashion trends.

Empathy

More than ever, a key focus for businesses has become engaging customers in meaningful relationships. Powerful brands, such as Nordstrom, American Express, and Zappos, have demonstrated that customer service can be an inimitable source of sustainable competitive advantage, not just another cost.

New metrics such as Net Promoter Score and Customer Effort Score indicate renewed interest in customer perceptions and have achieved such popularity that new companies have emerged to help businesses measure and track these scores.

Too many businesses approach customer service from a purely systems perspective and overlook the need for human engagement through empathy; what results is a façade of customer centricity, rather than truly outstanding service that people will pay a premium for, keep returning to, and extolling on social media.

To achieve a fundamental change in how they provide service, businesses must bring about a cultural change at every level of their organization. Companies renowned for customer service are not generally praised for their service center KPIs, but for their humanity and spontaneity.

It is often thought that customer service is about fixing things and solving problems; its real goal is to provide a positive experience that people identify with your company. Solving a customer's problem may achieve this, but can fall outside the scope of service personnel, for example, if the problem is escalated. When a customer reaches out for service, he or she wants to be heard and feel truly understood. *Customer service cannot always deliver solutions, but it can always deliver empathy.* The impact of customer emotions is vital in the service process. Customers who contact support maybe at the end of their tether, and the service desk maybe a last hope.

The difference between a good service experience and bad one stems from the level of empathy established by the service personnel; too often, they do not even ask the customer's name, which gives the message that they do not care about the individual.

How Innovation Can Engage and Delight Customers

Innovation is covered in greater depth in the final chapter, but it is worth noting here that when an organization can introduce an element of freshness to the product or service offering, they are adding value to what the customer buys.

Innovation is not limited to the introduction of new products, but may relate to service provision and the overall customer experience. New approaches to managing some of the processes can make life easier for the customer, so again, add value to the overall service offering.

Service Recovery

Mistakes are an unavoidable part of every service. Even the best service companies cannot prevent the occasional late flight, burnt steak, or missed delivery. As services are often performed in the customer's presence, errors are inevitable and evident to the customer.

So, while preventing all problems may not be realistic, companies can learn to recover from them. A good recovery can turn angry, frustrated customers into loyal ones, creating more goodwill than if things had gone smoothly in the first place. It is one of the most important elements of customer service, and it can make the difference between success and failure for any organization.

At his wife's request, Bob stopped at the Olive Garden Italian Restaurant in Bloomington, Minnesota, to pick up a salad to have with dinner that night. Upon opening the container, they found the dressing for which the Olive Garden is famous missing.

When Bob returned to the restaurant, the manager was waiting. He apologized profusely and gave Bob two bottles of dressing, a large dessert, and a 10 U.S. dollar gift card, enabling Bob and his wife to enjoy their salad and dessert and look forward to using their gift certificate.

They also told friends about the incident—glossing over the mistake, and focusing on what the manager had done to make up for it. The actual cost of what the manager gave to Bob and his wife was negligible; the word-of-mouth advertising the Olive Garden received for it was priceless.

Service recovery turns a negative situation around leaving the customer feeling he or she has just done business with the greatest company in the world. Word-of-mouth advertising is the most powerful advertising you can get—and it costs you nothing. Most of us, before making a purchasing decision, ask friends and co-workers for referrals. What they say is very influential, because they are people we know and whose opinions we trust.

On the flip side, people who have unresolved problems with a company tell anyone who will listen about their negative experience, often via social network, before leaving your premises.

Opportunities for service recovery abound. Any problem that employees can discover and resolve is a chance to go beyond the call of duty and win a customer for life. These are not the stuff of major disasters, but niggling mistaken billings and late deliveries, the seemingly small issues that can ignite a person's temper.

Addressing problems and preventing them from happening again can save money, as well as retain customers. Good recoveries from service problems usually happen because some exceptional individual takes the initiative to solve a customer's problem. Companies should take steps to ensure that everyone in the organization has the skill, motivation, and authority to make service recovery an integral part of operations.

The Road to Service Recovery

Service companies must be flexible and regain their balance instantly after a slipup. An obsession with the goal of customer satisfaction, adopting a customer-focused attitude, can help cultivate the special skills necessary to recovery.

Recovery skills often present greater challenge to companies that espouse TQM and pride themselves on having streamlined and efficient service delivery systems. They have rigid systems to ensure zero defects, sophisticated technologies and strict policies to control employee behavior, to ensure that even uneducated, unmotivated workers can

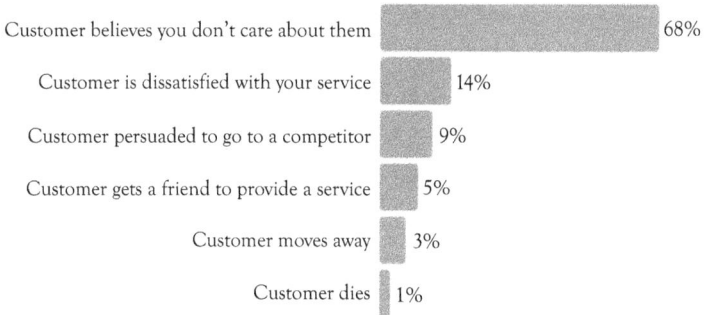

Customer believes you don't care about them	68%
Customer is dissatisfied with your service	14%
Customer persuaded to go to a competitor	9%
Customer gets a friend to provide a service	5%
Customer moves away	3%
Customer dies	1%

Figure 5.9 Why customers leave reproduced with kind permission of the Institute of Customer Service UK

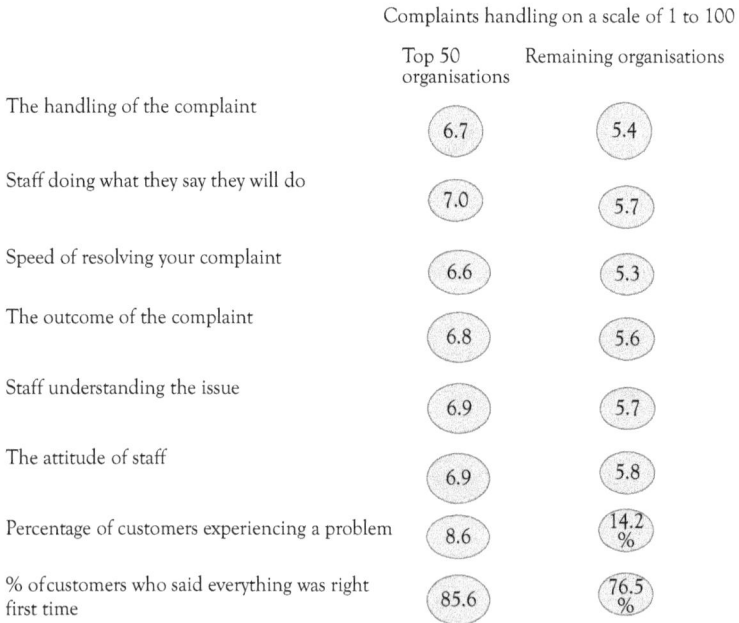

Complaints handling on a scale of 1 to 100

	Top 50 organisations	Remaining organisations
The handling of the complaint	6.7	5.4
Staff doing what they say they will do	7.0	5.7
Speed of resolving your complaint	6.6	5.3
The outcome of the complaint	6.8	5.6
Staff understanding the issue	6.9	5.7
The attitude of staff	6.9	5.8
Percentage of customers experiencing a problem	8.6	14.2%
% of customers who said everything was right first time	85.6	76.5%

Figure 5.10 Customer complaint handling adapted from the Institute of Customer Service UK

consistently deliver high-quality service. These production-based service delivery systems have gone a long way toward achieving consistently high service standards, but in services, no matter how rigorous the procedures and employee training or how advanced the technology, zero defects are an unattainable goal. Manufacturers that can adjust the inputs and machinery until products are uniformly perfect, but for service companies, variation is unavoidable. The weather and customers themselves are beyond a company's control and may adversely impact the service delivery. No system can ensure a plane can fly if fog comes down.

When problems arise, customers are almost always disappointed. Service delivery systems are designed to cater for normal conditions, not exceptions. Often, efforts to address customer complaints make the situation worse.

Empowering frontline workers to identify and solve the customer's problem is the best route, but this is counter to many companies' policies as it often involves rule breaking. Workers are trained not to alter the routine. They might like to help the customer, but are frustrated that they are not allowed to do it, or do not know how. Meanwhile, customers are frustrated and dissatisfied.

Companies should complement their systems with an equal facility for service recovery, making them as comfortable with the exceptions as they are with planned activity. Building skills to spots chances for service recovery, and going the extra mile is clearly an effort, but one well worth making.

Companies that want to build the capability of recovering from service problems should: measure the costs of effective service recovery, listen closely for complaints, anticipate needs for recovery, act fast, train employees, empower the front line, and close the customer feedback loop.

Customer Perceptions of Service

A recent United Kingdom survey by a customer service institute found the top scoring organization to be Amazon, with a customer satisfaction score of 87.3, an increase on its score in 2016. However, reports of poor staff relations in its fulfillment centers abound. It uses monitoring

quality
simple **helpful** reliable service
great **fast** fun
quick easy good
pleasant
professional **friendly** value **efficient**
convenient cheap
happy nice

Figure 5.11 Words, thoughts, and feelings customers use for the top 50 organizations reproduced with kind permission of the Institute of Customer Service UK. (https://instituteofcustomerservice.com/media/pdf/ukcsi-january-2017-1653.pdf)

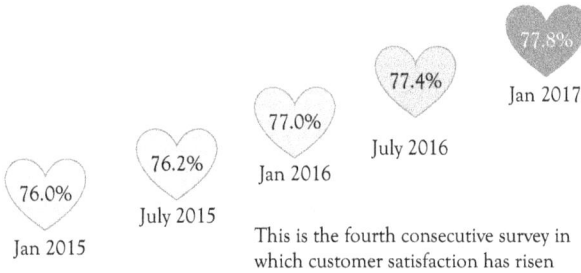

77.8%
Jan 2017

77.4%
July 2016

77.0%
Jan 2016

76.2%
July 2015

76.0%
Jan 2015

This is the fourth consecutive survey in which customer satisfaction has risen

Figure 5.12 Customer perceptions of service over time adapted from The Institute of Customer Service UK. (https://instituteof customerservice.com/media/pdf/ukcsi-january-2017-1653.pdf)

technologies to track employee performance in settings beyond the assembly line. Amazon claims "We make sure that every associate at Amazon is really a customer centric person, that cares about the customer." But, customers dislike staff to be badly treated, and such a focus on a time and motion style of management is likely to reduce Amazon's popularity.

Quotations or Interviews from key Practitioners and Leaders of Excellence Businesses

The key is to set realistic customer expectations, and then not to just meet them, but to exceed them - preferably in unexpected and helpful ways.

—Richard Branson

The first step in exceeding your customer's expectations is to know those expectations.

—Roy H Williams

Meeting expectations is good. Exceeding expectations is better.

—Ron Kaufman

Don't expect a great day; create one.

—Bob Procter

Enchantment Example

Booths North West U.K.-based farmshop or supermarket • Sells great-quality niche products, enjoyable shopping environment • Offers free coffee to members • Helpful and knowledgeable staff • Confidence in the expertise of product buyers • Booths display their links to the Cumbrian landscape through their use of Lakeland slate in the construction of the pillars. Fresh, seasonal plants create a welcome and a promise of good things inside	

Disenchantment Example

	British Telecom A communication company that is hard to communicate with, and that rewards new customers and hiked the prices for loyal customers.

Pictures of Excellence

A gentle, intellectual wit appeals to the customer demographic of Booths Supermarkets—a chain of 28 high-end supermarkets in select areas of Northern England. The display has a clever pun that echoes the witticisms on the bags themselves. Bags are offered in a variety of colors, and many customers use them as handbags, as well as for their shopping

The chain is taking advantage of the recent legal requirement for U.K. supermarkets to charge for carrier bags, and the customer base of Booths is sufficiently environmentally aware to purchase reusable shopping bags.

This represents a great way for customers to express their advocacy, as well as displaying their green credentials and sense of humor.

End of Chapter Summary

This chapter has covered some of the aspects that make service delivery really great fun for customers and staff alike. Although there are frameworks that can help to structure this, ultimately, much of the success in delighting customers is derived from recruiting people with the right kind of attitudes, empowering them to use their initiative, and being willing to bend the rules on occasion.

Systems can go part of the way to ensuring smooth service provision, without hitches, but that is unlikely to take customers beyond mere satisfaction. Delight is likely to be achieved as the result of someone in the company doing something exceptional. This is one key area in which the philosophy element of service excellence plays an essential role.

End of Chapter Review Questions

Exceeding customer expectations

Question	Strongly agree	Agree	Neither agree nor disagree	Disagree	Strongly disagree
We have a clear understanding of our customers' explicit expectations (mental targets for product performance, such as well-identified performance standards)					
We have a clear understanding of our customers' implicit expectations. An implicit expectation might be relative "Compared with other companies..." or "Compared to the leading brand..."					
We have a clear understanding of performance expectations related to the quality of outcome (may include the evaluation of accessibility, customization, dependability, timeliness, accuracy, and user-friendly interfaces).					
We understand customer expectations of dynamic performance (how the product or service is expected to evolve over time—the changes in support, product, or service needed to meet future business or use environments).					

We understand customer expectations of technology performance (not just feature based, but technology that enhances perceptions of status, ego, self-image).					
We understand interpersonal customer					
expectations that reflect the relationship between the customer and product or service provider.					
We understand how situations alter customer expectations (purchase stages, purpose of purchase, and so on).					
We actively look for opportunities to delight our customers.					
Our frontline staff are empowered to deal with service recovery issues, even if it means they have to bend the rules.					

Adapted from Smith, S 2018 Types of customer expectations.

References

https://bbc.com/news/magazine-26468295

http://customer-service.com/blog/201202/Service-Recovery-Four-Steps-to-Increasing-Customer-Loyalty

https://instituteofcustomerservice.com/media/pdf/ukcsi-january-2017-1653.pdf

http://salon.com/2014/02/23/worse_than_wal_mart_amazons_sick_brutality_and_secret_history_of_ruthlessly_intimidating_workers/

https://slideshare.net/RightNow/2010-customer-experience-impact

https://biz30.timedoctor.com/exceptional-customer-service-that-can-make-any-business-profitable/

https://hbr.org/1990/07/the-profitable-art-of-service-recoveryukcsi-jan17-state-of-the-nation-report-online-1676.pdf

About the Author

Fiona Urquhart MBA, FCIM, FIC, from a grounding in retail with the John Lewis Partnership, Fiona gained an MBA from CASS Business School. She is currently MBA Module Leader for Durham University on Service Excellence Design, and previously taught for the Open University. She gained experience of applied marketing innovation work, developing AC Nielsen's EPOS-based research service, Scantrack, and a pilot EFTPOS service with a consortium of the retail clearing banks.

Fiona now provides consultancy support to diverse service and manufacturing companies, as well as doing charitable work with start-up companies in the most deprived wards of Newcastle Upon Tyne. She also supports marketing and service excellence projects at various corporations, as well as delivering elements of degree apprenticeships for a number of infrastructure companies. In both her teaching work and her corporate training work she has developed expertise in problem-based learning to create practical learning situations and encourage reflective learning. She has delivered a series of interactive workshops for several European universities to research the topic in the context of entrepreneurial learning and will be presenting her findings at a number of global conferences.

You can see more about Fiona here https://linkedin.com/in/fionaurquhart1/

Index

Note: '*f*' after page number refers to figure and '*t*' after page number refers to table.

Allegiant Air, 87, 88
Alnwick Studio, 77
Amazon, 131
American Airlines, 88
The American Marketing Association, 14
Apple, 25

Bain and Company, 32
Bennis, Warren, 99
Brand activation
definition, 91
strategies for, 92–93
Brand association, 34–36
basis for, 36
Brand authenticity
and customers, 27
definition, 27
key components in, 27–28
role of information in, 93–95, 121
Brand backstory
creation of, 30
importance of, 29
meaning, 29
Brand designing, 18
Brand elements, 34*f*, 35*t*
criteria for, 34–37, 35*t*
Brand equity. *See also* Brand trust
definition, 36
as customer perspective, 36–37, 131–132
Brand naming
name characteristics, 24–25
name types, 22–23
Brand prism, 21*f*
elements of, 21–22
Brand refreshing, need for, 40
Brand trust. *See also* Customer involvement

attributes, 72*t*
and brand activation, 91–92
components, 76*f*
creating, 89–91
Edelman trust index, 72
enemies of, 88–89
importance, 69–70, 75
information as a determinant of, 72–73, 93–94
internal branding, 73–75, 83
organizational trust, 71–72
and pricing influence, 86–87
role of e-commerce on, 95–98
role of feedback in, 83–85
role of service recovery in, 98
trust and purchase involvement, 84–86
Brand values, 28
approaches to, 26, 28–29
core-values in, 26–27
importance of, 25–26
Brand, 13. *See also* Brand trust; Service excellence
action points for, 22
authenticity, 27–28
backstory, 29–32
and brand prism, 19*f*, 20–21
brand pyramid model, 19*f*
customer relationship, 13, 15, 21, 22, 29, 32–33, 50, 53, 54, 70, 95*f*, 98, 114, 127
definition, 14, 15
designing, key aspects in, 18
elements, 33–37
and employer branding, 38–40
Kapferer model, the, 19
Keller model, the, 19
key objective for, 17
key questions for creating, 13–14

and loyalty loop, 15–17
name characteristics, 24–25
name types, 22–23
refreshing, 40–43
role of, 14–15
strategies, 13
values, 25–27
Branson, Richard, 132
British Petroleum (BP), 77
Buffett, Warren, 99
Business orientation, 5

Capitol Records, 94
Corporate Social Responsibility
    (CSR), 76
Customer delight, 3, 4
Customer expectations. *See also*
    Employee performance;
    Service provision
communication for, 112, 121
customer elements in 125–126
and empathy, 127–128
importance of processes in meeting,
    119–120
importance of, 108
mapping customer touchpoints,
    113–114
meeting expectations, 109–111
memorable service, 113
priority areas for, 111–114
role of customer input, 126–127
service quality *vs.* speed, 111–112
staff role in meeting, 114–116
understanding customer,
    108–109
Customer insights, 56
Customer involvement
customer rage, 122
definition, 71
levels of, 71, 109
role of customer input, 126–127
trust and purchase involvement,
    84–86
types, 71
Customer journey mapping, 55–56
Customer lifetime value (CLV), 110
Customer loyalty, 30, 33, 49, 52–53,
    96, 110. *See also* Brand
categories, 17

as loop model, 15–17
and lovemark, 17, 68
Customer mix, 108, 123
definition, 121
management of, 121–122
Customer personas, 54–55, 123
Customer rage, 122
Customersure, 33
Customer touchpoint, 43, 45–46,
    50, 55, 86, 113–114. *See also*
    Customer involvement
categories of, 55, 70
involvement levels, 71
Customer-to-customer interactions
    (CCI), 121
Customer-to-employee interactions
    (CEI), 121

Decision-making, 15, 17
Delta, 88

EasyJet, 88
E-commerce. *See also* Brand trust
and customer loyalty, 96, 111
and e-trust, 96
online store image factors, 96
website design parameters,
    96–98
Edelman trust index, 72
EEEEEEE model, 6
Employee performance
in customer expectations, 112
differentiators for, 114, 115*f*
goal achievement, 114
performance appraisals, 114,
    115–116
role of leaders in, 116–119
role of positive work environment
    for, 115
Employer branding. *See also* Internal
    branding *under* brand trust
approaches to, 39–40
importance of, 38–39
Experience economy, 124
Extended marketing mix, 45–46

Feefo, 33, 60, 84
Ford, Henry, 61
Frontier, 86

Gaps model, 57. *See also*
    SERVQUAL model
Gates, Bill, 61
Gray, Chris, 87

Honore, Russell, 98
Hsieh, Tony, 62

Internal branding, 74, 83

Jobs, Steve, 25
Jubelirer, Michelle, 94

Kapferer, Jean Noel, 19
Kapferer model, 19, 20
    brand prism model, 21*f*
Kaufman, Ron, 131
Keller, Kevin Lane, 19, 34
Keller model, 19
    brand resonance pyramid, 19*f,*
        19–20
King, Chris, 62

Leadership
    good *vs.* outstanding, 117*f*
    importance of, 116, 118
    servant leadership, 119
Lovemark, 17, 20

Management theory, 4–5
Mercer, David, 3
McKinsey, 15, 17, 32
Mercedes Benz, 20
Microsoft, 61
Mode, 94
Moments of truth, 50
    definition of, 54
    identifying, 54–56
        customer insights, 56, 121
        customer journey mapping,
            55–56
        customer personas, 54–55, 109
        role of marketing in, 54
Morgan, Gareth, 3
Musk, Elon, 61

NetPromoter, 33
Net Promoter Score (NPS), 60

Olay, 94
Organizational trust. *See also* Brand
    trust
    attributes, 72t
    components of, 76*f*
    definition, 71–72
    role of feedback in, 83–84

Parcelforce, 75
PayPal, 61
Perceived risk, 70, 85
Procter, Bob, 133

Ryanair, 88
Reicheld, Frederick, 32
Roberts, Kevin, 17
Robinson, Lily, 62–64
Robson and Sons, 29–30

Saatchi, 17
Selfridge, Henry, 61
Servant leadership, 119
Service excellence, 4, 30, 83. *See also*
        Brand; Brand trust; Service
        quality
    application of, 1
    attributes of, 3
    benefits of, 8–9
    customer needs, 4, 108–109
    and customer service, 1–2, 3*f,* 7,
        53, 59–60, 98, 109, 114, 119
    EEEEEEE model, 6
    empathy in, 127–128
    iceberg, 2*f*
    meaning, 1, 9
    mission, 4
    processes in, 4, 6
    role of customer in, 2, 49, 54, 95*f,*
        98, 123, 126–127
    role of experience economy in,
        124–125
    role of innovation in, 128
    7 Es of, 6*f*
    SWOT analysis in, 2
    truisms in, 7
Service profit chain, 52*f*
Service provision
    customer training guidelines,
        123–124

experience economy, 124–125
importance of customer in, 122
Service quality
    awards and feedbacks, 60, 83–84
    costs of poor quality, 52, 53
    customer relationship, 50, 114
    and customer touchpoint, 42, 44*t*,
        45, 50, 55, 86, 113–114
    definition, 51
    designing of, 53, 59–60
    goals, 49–50
    importance of, 51–53
    measurement of, 57–58
    moments of truth, 50, 54–56
    and service profit chain, 52*f*
    SERVQUAL model, the, 57–58
    sum of all benefits, 50
Service recovery, 98, 128–129
    steps to, 129, 131
Service theater model, 122
Service, 1, 51, 53, 98, 107, 109, 114,
        119, 121, 122. *See also* Service
        excellence; Service provision;
        Service quality; Service
        recovery
    and electronic record, 1, 22
    excellence, 1, 2
    good *vs.* bad, 1, 52–53, 128
    as a performance, 125
Service theater model, 122
Servicescape, 122, 123
SERVQUAL model, the, 57
    customer-service design, 59–60
    dimensions of, 58
Servuction model, the, 122–123
Shell, 93

Sound managerial processes, 3–4
SpaceX, 61
Spirit, 87, 88
Staubach, Roger, 99
SurveyMonkey, 33

Tesco, 78
Tesla, 61
Tom's Shoes, 30, 31*t*
Total Quality Management (TQM),
        108, 119, 130
    definition, 119
    importance of processes in,
        119–120
    principles in, 120
Touchpoints, 70–71
TQM. *See* Total Quality Management
Trader joe's delivers, 83–84
TripAdvisor, 84, 86
Trustpilot, 60, 84

Unilever, 18
U.S. Airways, 88

Volkswagen, 85*f*–86*f*
Volvo, 91–92

Walmart, 65
Whirlpool, 65–66
Whizz Air, 88
Williams, Roy H., 133
Williams Holdings, 37

Ziglar, Zig, 98
Zappos, 62

OTHER TITLES IN OUR SERVICE SYSTEMS AND INNOVATIONS IN BUSINESS AND SOCIETY COLLECTION

Jim Spohrer, IBM and Haluk Demirkan, Arizona State University, Editors

- *Service Design with Applications to Health Care Institutions* by Oscar Barros
- *How Can Digital Technologies Improve Public Services and Governance?* by Nagy K. Hanna
- *The Accelerating TechnOnomic Medium ('ATOM'): It's Time to Upgrade the Economy* by Kartik Gada
- *Sustainability and the City: The Service Approach* by Adi Wolfson
- *Everything Old is New Again: How Entrepreneurs Use Discourse Themes to Reclaim Abandoned Urban Spaces* by Miriam Plavin-Masterman
- *The Interconnected Individual: Seizing Opportunity in the Era of AI, Platforms, Apps, and Global Exchanges* by Hunter Hastings and Jeff Saperstein
- *T-Shaped Professionals: Adaptive Innovators* by Yassi Moghaddam, Haluk Demirkan, and Jim Spohrer
- *The Value Imperative* by Gautam Mahajan
- *Virtual Local Manufacturing Communities: Online Simulations of Future Workshop Systems* by William Sims Bainbridge

Announcing the Business Expert Press Digital Library

Concise e-books business students need for classroom and research

This book can also be purchased in an e-book collection by your library as

- a one-time purchase,
- that is owned forever,
- allows for simultaneous readers,
- has no restrictions on printing, and
- can be downloaded as PDFs from within the library community.

Our digital library collections are a great solution to beat the rising cost of textbooks. E-books can be loaded into their course management systems or onto students' e-book readers. The **Business Expert Press** digital libraries are very affordable, with no obligation to buy in future years. For more information, please visit **www.businessexpertpress.com/librarians**. To set up a trial in the United States, please email **sales@businessexpertpress.com**.